# Beyond Crystal Do
# - a Workbook

Simon and Sue Lilly

Tree Seer Publications

# Beyond Crystal Doorways
# - a Workbook



ISBN 1-905454-05-8/ ISBN 978-1905454-05-1



Design by Sue Lilly

Published by: Tree Seer Publications
PO Box 6
Exminster, Exeter, Devon, EX6 8YE
Tel: 01392 832005
Email: info@greenmanshop.co.uk
Web: www.greenmanshop.co.uk

# Contents

# GUIDELINES FOR USING NETS.

When using a crystal net it is important to follow some guidelines:-

1) Always allow yourself plenty of space and time - never squeeze a crystal net in between other appointments. It is always advisable to take several minutes to settle down and focus on how you feel before lying down in the net. This will allow the possibility of clearer experiences and the ability to notice changes more easily.

2) Different people will experience different sensations in the nets depending on their energy patterns. Experience will probably differ from one session to another, again depending on the individual's energies and those of the environment.

3) If you are very tired - you are more likely to fall asleep than experience anything. Unless, of course, your reason for entering a net is either to fall asleep or to wake yourself up!

4) At first it is often only by contrast that you will notice changes between how you feel in and out of the net. It is always better to spend a short time regularly in the net than spend a long time occasionally.

5) The maximum time we suggest you stay in any one net is twenty minutes. (Don't worry if you accidentally go over this time, however). We find that the experience deepens every four or five minutes. there is a definite shift of energy, a sinking to a new level. So the natural finishing times are five, ten, fifteen and twenty minutes or thereabouts. You will soon get used to the feel of the end of one period and the beginning of another as there is a tendency to "float back up to the surface" before the next dive begins. It is less of a jar to the system to end a session as you are moving outwards towards ordinary consciousness than to break while on an inwards/downward arc.

6) Always take time to come round to everyday activity slowly. Ideally you should have twice the time you have been in the net before you need to do anything focused. This will give the body time to integrate the energies it has experienced into its

normal everyday functioning.
Allow any feelings of impatience, fidgeting or restlessness to disappear BEFORE you resume normal activity.

7) Make sure that you will not be disturbed while you are in the net and during the rest period afterwards.

8) If at any time you feel discomfort or anxiety whilst in the net, quietly get up and find somewhere to relax until the sensations disappear. Re-enter the net or end the session and remain relaxing for a while.

9) There are several crystal layouts which can be used before or after using a crystal net. A few minutes, (between five and ten minutes) will be sufficient to rebalance energies.

9a For initial balancing and calming:
Place a clear quartz point outwards at the crown of the head, rose quartz at the heart and smoky quartz, point downwards, close to the base of the spine.

9b For disorientation or "feeling out of sorts" clear quartz at crown of head, lapis lazuli or turquoise at the centre of the forehead and a smoky quartz between the legs close to the spine.

9c For grounding, bringing down to earth, back to reality:
smoky quartz at the throat, just above the collar bones, and smoky quartz at the base of spine, between the legs.

10) Unless specified otherwise all crystal nets should be laid out so that the head is aligned with magnetic north. This places the individual's bioelectromagnetic field in harmony with the flow of the earth's energy field.

11) Drinking a little pure water before and after each crystal net session can help both with the removal of toxicity often released and with the integration of new information and experience.

12) It is very important that all crystals used in these nets are cleansed before and after use. This ensures that any residual disharmonies are removed from the stone. There are many different ways to

cleanse crystals:

a) hold the crystals under running water for a couple of minutes and allow to dry naturally
b) pass the crystals through incense smoke or smudge
c) place inside a resonant sound source - singing bowl, bell
d) wipe with pennyroyal or quartz essence

13) Keep a piece of paper and pen handy for when you finish. Make notes, drawings, scribbles, of your experiences as soon as you leave the net. Otherwise you will forget the more subtle aspects of your experience. If you "hear" words or phrases these can often be the quickest to disappear or change. Write them down as you remember them - interpret later, at your leisure.

14) It can be interesting to begin by experiencing one net, followed by another, to notice the differences i.e. Moon followed by Mercury.

15) If you don't have a cloth of the preferred colour to lie on, then use a white cloth, or a white cloth with a colour filter, colour tincture or light essence.

16) Some "netters" experience a welter of visual imagery whilst others are focused more on how they feel emotionally or sensations in the body. None is "better" than the other, different people translate the energy shifts in terms or language they are familiar with.
Sometimes the kinesthetic (feeling) person gets a clearer idea what a net is about—visual imagery, like dream images, need some interpretation.
It can take more sessions to identify a pattern in the types of image presented. Ideally a good balance of all the senses will give the fullest experience. So if you do favour one sense try to spend some time in a net focusing on the others. If you are visual, get used to feeling how the body is, what your mood is; if you are kinesthetic, watch your thoughts carefully.

## So Why Stars?

Why should we be interested in phenomena that are so far away from us and our lives?
Well, firstly, just because something is at a great distance doesn't mean that we do not feel, at some level, its influence. Planetary influences are largely measurable by the effects they have on the life cycles of living beings. Yet, to our human perceptions, the only difference between stars and planets is that the planets appear to wander around the sky. Stars are called 'fixed' because they do not show this peculiarity. They remain in set relationships as they all seem to swing together in great arcs across the night sky.

Our perceptions of the stars are very different from those of our ancestors of even a couple of hundred years ago. We now see them as very remote, physical phenomena and define stars in terms of inconceivable dimensions both in size and distance that make no real sense to our everyday experience.
The sheer vastness of space all around us, although brought nearer by equipment that can magnify and identify energies we cannot see, does not bring the reality any closer. Astronomy and astro-physics simply create a new cosmology, a new imaginative construct of the reality of 'outer space' of which we feel we have little participation. How can an object so many millions, million miles away affect my life when even the light from that star is millions of years old when we see it in the sky?

We do experience stars, we do sense them even in a way that is deeper and more present than many of the nearer planets. And this is why it is a big mistake to conclude that because something has a small influence, then that influence must be unimportant.

When we look at a star, we interact with that star. Its light, no matter how old it may be, is a really present experience. It interacts in a physical way with our eyes, our brain, our cells. Light communicates. In fact, light has been found to be the way in which living structures communicate and interact with each other. The model of chemical and electrical interactions of cells has given way to the understanding that chemical and electrical phenomena within cells is simply a means of modifying bioluminescence—very low levels of light emissions that flash almost instantaneously through the body transmitting information. In much the same way, in fact, as stars can be seen to flicker and flash in the night sky!

When we see something, we sense it. Our biological evolution has determined a use for that perception. Starlight is less a part of our lives today (in a conscious manner) than at any other time in human history. Lifestyles and technology wipe away our experience of stars and starlight. Light pollution and high atmospheric pollution dim the sky so that even if we do remember to look up from the flickering computer or television screens, we rarely see much at all.

Throughout history and probably pre-history, stars have been the visible presence of the spirit worlds, mysterious, numinous, incomprehensible to most but nonetheless, present and very real.

During the long years of the Mesopotamian city states and culminating in Babylon, careful observation of the stars was correlated with events over a long period of time on earth. This was the development of astrology as we understand its systems today. But even thousands of years before this humans were watching and noticing the cycles of stars rising and falling with the sharp eyes of hunters who have learnt not to ignore even the smallest of signs in their surroundings.

Starlight is a primeval factor in our psyche. The fact that we now place unworldly characteristics on stars really just emphasises in the same respect their huge importance. Despite the distances, despite the spans of aeons, despite the mythical physics of fission and fusion, super novae and 'red dwarfs', stars impinge on our lives and as such exploring their energetic and experiential effects can be of value. From a single exploration viewpoint, what could be more fascinating than travelling so far, of going beyond time into the distant past, whilst still remaining here in the present?

The influence of stars—both planets and fixed stars—was clearly demonstrated by the Babylonian priesthood who formulated the models of astrology by astronomical observation. Light is the means whereby life communicates with itself. So starlight will inevitably play a role in our personal well-being. Each star has its own light, its own message and if the information a star gives us is what we are needing in our lives—in our functioning health or in our spiritual nutrition—then working with the appropriate star nets can provide access to the energy that we require.

For those interested in astrology, where a fixed star coincides with planets in a natal chart, working with the net of that star can be very useful to create profound healing and integration of energies at a soul level.

Simon & Sue
August 2007

# Fixed Star Doorways

# Achenar

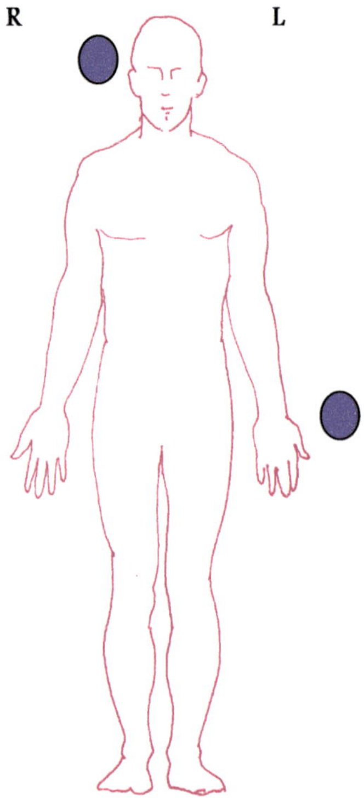


**Crystals needed:**
2 amethysts

**Colour of cloth to lie on:**
Pink

**Placement of Stones**
Place one amethyst beside the Sacral chakra, on the left side
Place one amethyst beside the Ajna (brow) chakra, on the right side

**What this net can be used for:**
Helping to cope with the stresses of being in positions of authority
Encourages opportunities
Increase in happiness and success

**Zodiac Position**
$15^{\circ}19$ Pisces

# Aldebaran



**Crystals needed:**
8 rose quartz

**Colour of cloth to lie on:**
Blue

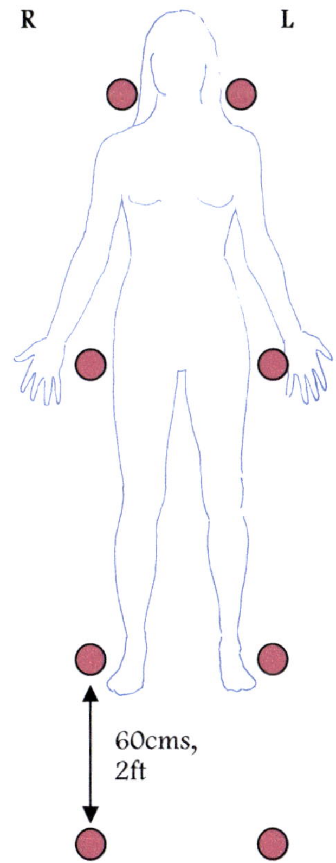


**Placement of Stones**
Place one rose quartz either side of the neck/shoulder
Place one rose quartz either side of the hip at a level of the base of the spine
Place one rose quartz beside each foot
Place one rose quartz about 60cms/2ft below the stone by the feet

**What this net can be used for:**
Linking to the energy of Archangel Michael
Helps you to deal with many tasks at the same time
Eases difficulties when others are jealous of your success

**Zodiac Position**
9°47 Gemini

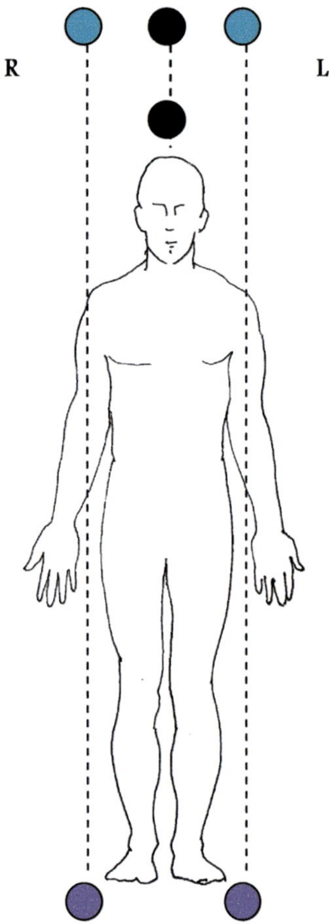


# Altair

**Crystals needed:**
2 black tourmaline
2 turquoise
2 amethyst

**Colour of cloth to lie on:**
Black

**Placement of Stones**
On the midline, just above the head—a black tourmaline
On the midline, above this stone—a second black tourmaline
Level with the second tourmaline, in line with the shoulders, two turquoise
In line with the turquoise, just below the level of the feet, two amethyst

**What this net can be used for:**
Helps to temper over-ambition
Enhances both imagination and logic
For looking into the depths of the Self

**Zodiac position**
1°47 Aquarius

# Antares

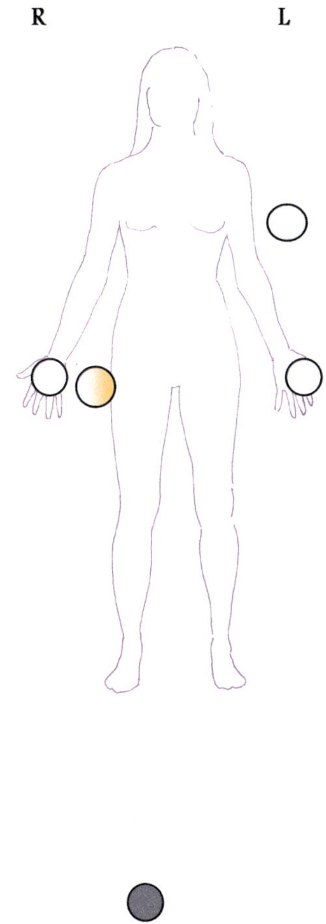


**Crystals needed:**
2 clear quartz
1 rutile quartz
1 moonstone
1 lodestone (magnetite)

**Colour of cloth to lie on:**
Violet/Purple

**Placement of Stones**
Level with the heart at the left side of the body a white moonstone
Level with the base of the spine on the right side of the body—rutile quartz
Place one clear quartz in each hand
Below the right foot at the level of the Earth Star chakra (approximately 1m ), place a lodestone/magnetite

**What this net can be used for:**
Easing irritability and hyperactivity
Balancing extremes of moods and behaviour
Breaking out of destructive patterns
Gathering energy and impetus for important activity
Linking to Archangel Uriel

**Zodiac Position**
9°46 Sagittarius

# Arcturus

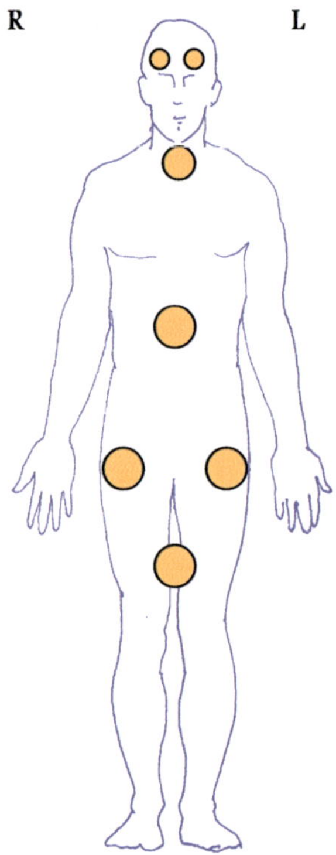


**Crystals needed:**
7 yellow quartz
(citrine/lemon quartz)

**Colour of cloth to lie on:**
Violet/Purple

**Placement of Stones**
Place one yellow quartz on both of the temporal lobes of the forehead
One yellow quartz at the base of the throat
One yellow quartz at the Solar Plexus chakra
One yellow quartz on the front of each hip bone
One yellow quartz at or near the base of the spine

**What this net can be used for:**
Supports efforts to gain recognition from hard work
Balances energies before and after psychic or occult work
Quietening personal energies to enable rest

**Zodiac Position**
24°14 Libra

# Beta Centauri/Agena

Crystals needed:
2 black tourmaline
1 rubellite (pink tourmaline)
1 clear quartz

Colour of cloth to lie on:
Yellow

Placement of Stones
Place one black tourmaline by the left hand
Place a clear quartz beside the left foot
Place the rubellite beside the right foot
Below the rubellite, (the same distance from the rubellite as the clear quartz) place the second black tourmaline

What this net can be used for:
Sharpening observation and mental acuity
Helping to bring success to creative projects
Enhancing the ability to socialise and be at ease with others

Zodiac Position
23°48 Scorpio

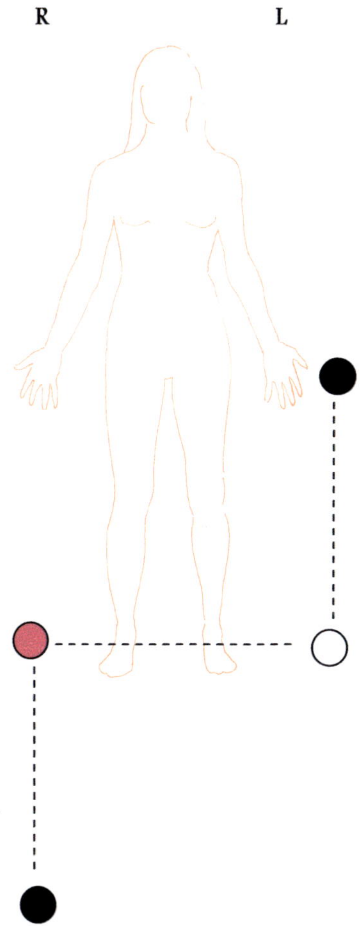

# Betelgeuse

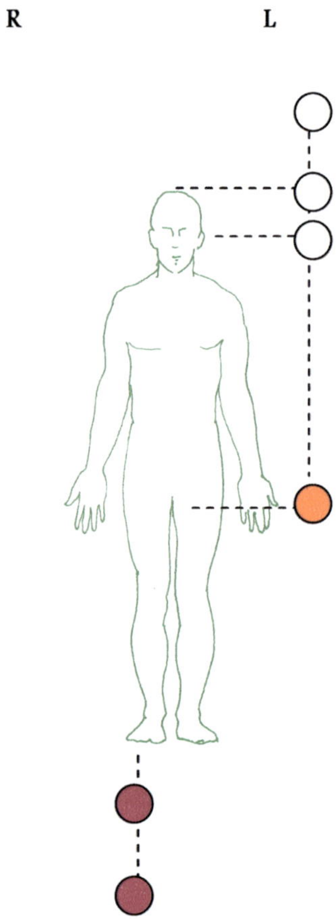


**Crystals needed:**
3 clear quartz
2 red garnet
1 carnelian

**Colour of cloth to lie on:**
Green

**Placement of Stones**
Four stones beside the left of the body in a straight line:
Clear quartz beside the ear
Clear quartz level with the top of the head
Clear quartz equidistant above this
Carnelian at the level of the base of the spine

One garnet under the right foot, away from the body
One garnet equidistant, below that

**What this net can be used for:**
Encouraging writing and communication
Initiating activity by removing blocks
Eases worries over success of projects

**Zodiac position**
28°45 Gemini

# Bungula (Alpha Centauri or Toliman)

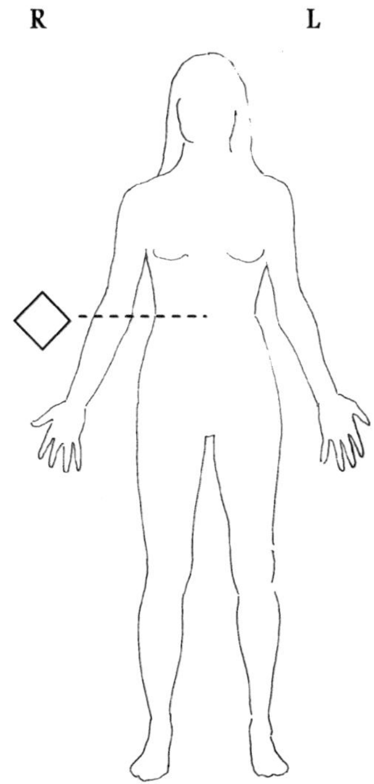


**Crystals needed:**
1 clear calcite
(preferably Iceland spar)

**Colour of cloth to lie on:**
Black

**Placement of Stones**
Place calcite on the right side, level with the Solar Plexus chakra

**What this net can be used for:**
Supporting people who are active in public life where their private life is suffering
Easing relationships with women
Helps to dissolve links to enemies or those who would do us harm

**Zodiac position**
29°29 Scorpio

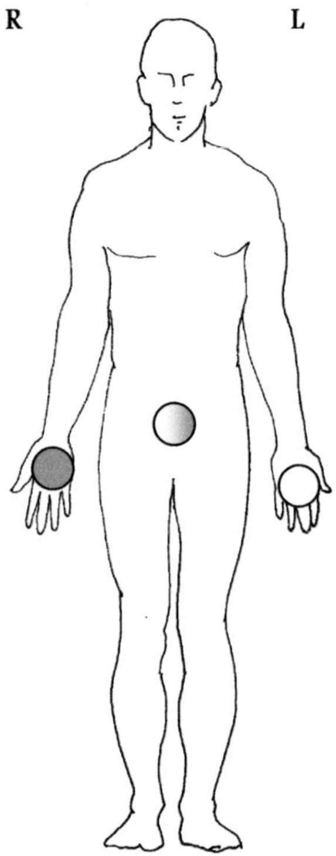


# Canopus

**Crystals needed:**
1 clear quartz
1 smoky quartz
1 selenite (clear gypsum)

**Colour of cloth to lie on:**
Black

**Placement of Stones**
Place the clear quartz in the left hand
Place the smoky quartz in the right hand
Place the selenite at the second chakra

**What this net can be used for:**
Helps to settle energies after travel
Encourages increase in self-worth and self-image
Broadens personal views and knowledge especially when it is difficult to put personal issues into context

**Zodiac position**
14°58 Cancer

# Deneb Adige



**Crystals needed:**
1 amethyst
2 red garnet

**Colour of cloth to lie on:**
Blue

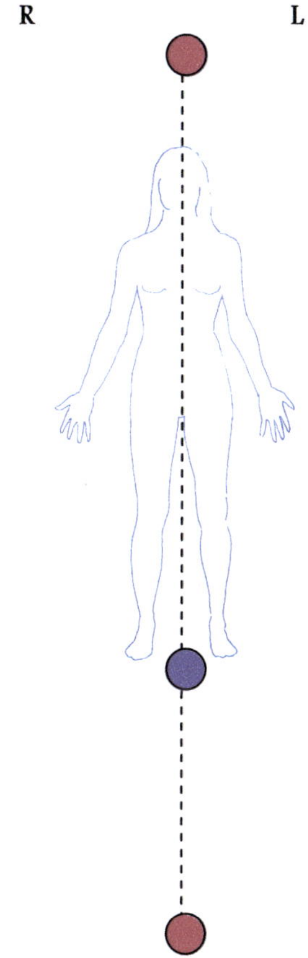


**Placement of Stones**
Place one garnet, midline 2 feet/40cms above the top of the head
Place the amethyst midline between the feet
Place one garnet midline below the amethyst, as far away from the body as the space will allow

**What this net can be used for:**
Enhancing creative skills
Speeding up the intellect and intuition
Supporting business endeavours

**Zodiac Position**
5°20 Pisces

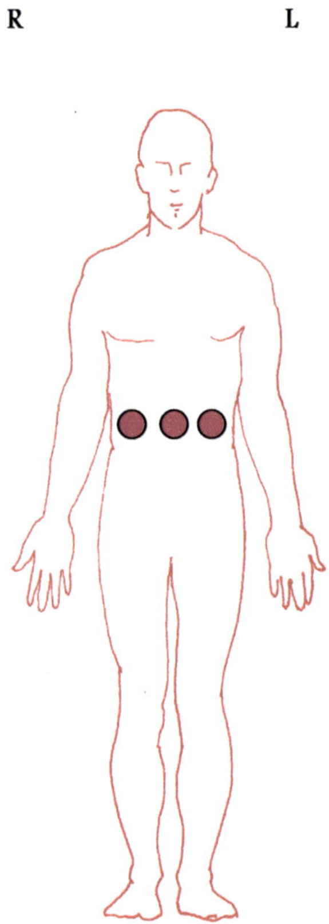


# Formalhaut

**Crystals needed:**
3 red garnets

**Colour of cloth to lie on:**
Red

**Placement of Stones**
3 red garnets in a line at the level of the Solar plexus

**What this net can be used for:**
Linking to Archangel Gabriel
Supports ambition in artistic pursuits
Helpful in anchoring imagination and inspiration for practical use

**Zodiac position**
$3^{o}52$ Pisces

# Pleiades

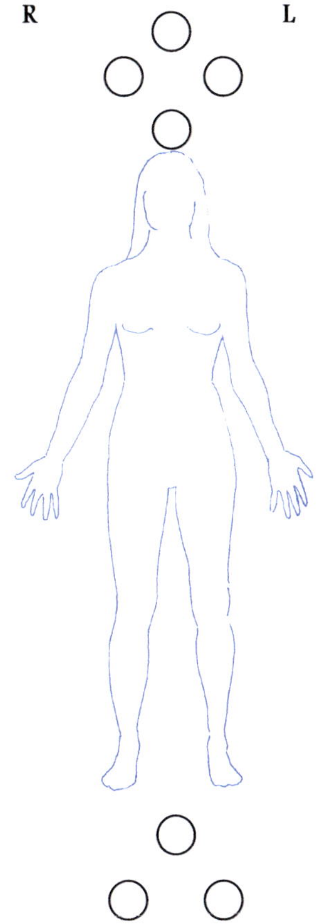


**Crystals needed:**
7 clear quartz

**Colour of cloth to lie on:**
Blue

**Placement of Stones**
Place one clear quartz just above the head on the midline
Place three clear quartz making a diamond shape above this stone
Place one clear quartz on the midline, just below the feet
Add two clear quartz shoulder-width apart below this making an equilateral triangle.

**What this net can be used for:**
Coping with times of change, especially involving grief
Encouraging new ideas
Linking with the Earth, protecting the planet

**Zodiac position**
29°25 Taurus to 0°23 Gemini

# Polaris

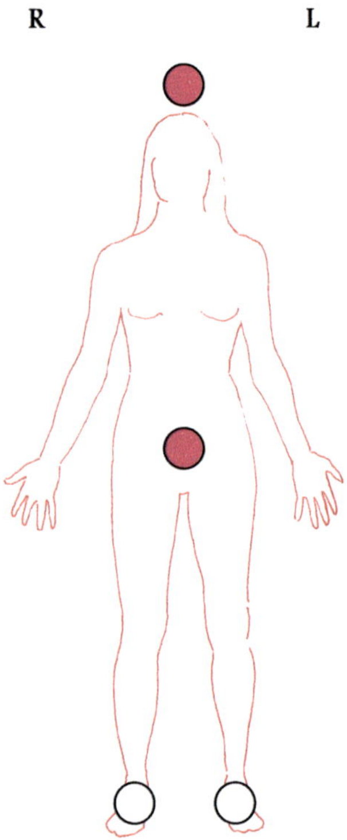


**Crystals needed:**
2 clear quartz
2 pink tourmaline
(rubellite)

**Colour of cloth to lie on:**
Red

**Placement of Stones**
Place one rubellite at the top of the head
Place one rubellite at the hara (2nd chakra)
Place a clear quartz at the arch on each foot

**What this net can be used for:**
Focusing on what is required and necessary
Encouraging the ability to manage any situation with ease
Maintaining spiritual direction, whatever occurs

**Zodiac position**
28°24 Gemini

# Procyon

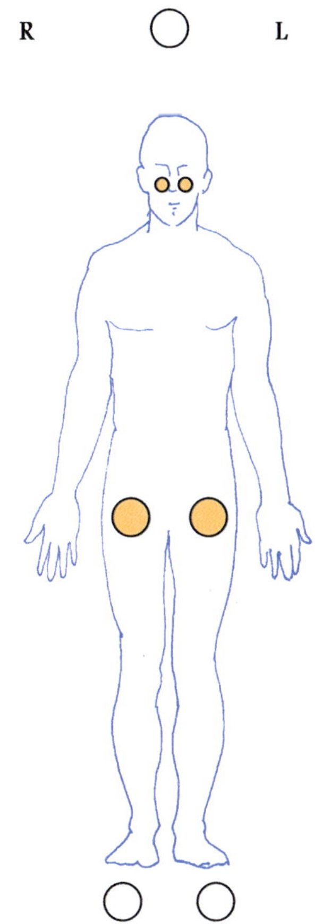


**Crystals needed:**
3 clear quartz
4 yellow citrine

**Colour of cloth to lie on:**
Blue

**Placement of Stones**
Place one clear quartz well above the head on the midline
Place a yellow citrine under each eye, on the cheekbones
Place a yellow citrine on the front of each hip bone
Place a clear quartz below each foot

**What this net can be used for:**
Eases feeling of anger and restlessness
Enables strong emotions to be used creatively
Enhances willpower and ability to take the initiative

**Zodiac position**
25°47 Cancer

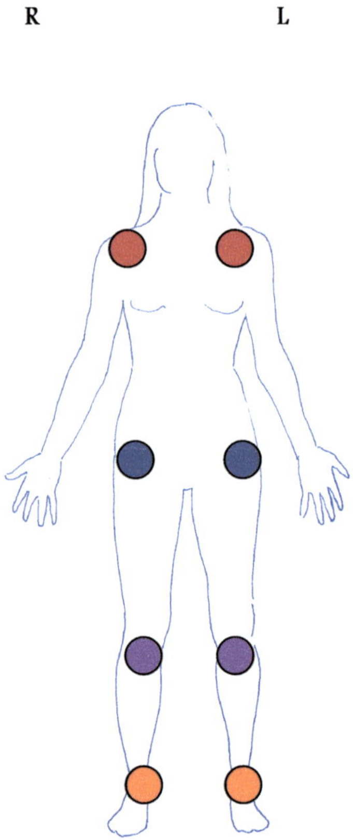


# Regulus

**Crystals needed:**
2 red jasper
2 lapis lazuli
2 amethyst
2 carnelian

**Colour of cloth to lie on:**
White

**Placement of Stones**
Place one red jasper at the front of each shoulder
Place one lapis lazuli on the front of each hip bone
Place one amethyst just below each knee cap
Place a carnelian at the front of each ankle where the leg joins the foot

**What this net can be used for:**
For linking with Archangel Raphael
Supporting advancement in life purpose
Aiding investigation and integration of the Shadow Self

**Zodiac position**
29°50 Leo

# Rigel

**Crystals needed:**
4 clear quartz

**Colour of cloth to lie on:**
Yellow

**Placement of Stones**
Four clear quartz placed in a square around the body
- either side and above the head
- either side and below the feet

**What this net can be used for:**
Tempering aggressive tendencies
Encouraging a balanced approach to service within a community
Skilful management of personal energies

**Zodiac position**
16°50 Gemini

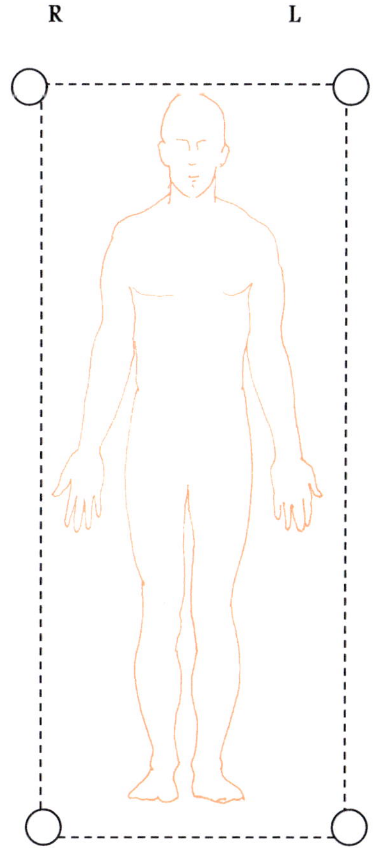

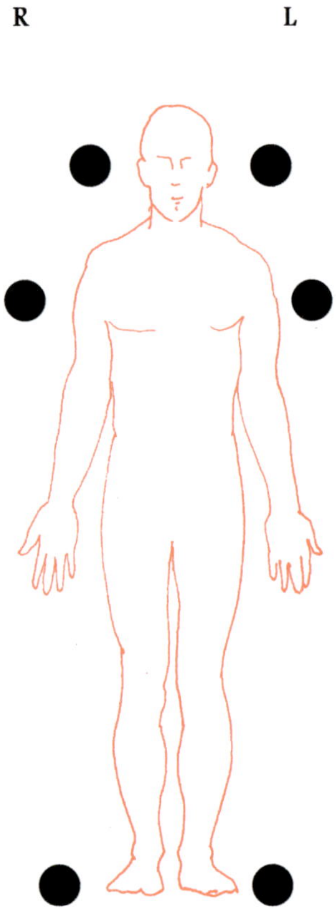


# Sirius

**Crystals needed:**
6 pieces of jet

**Colour of cloth to lie on:**
Orange

**Placement of Stones**
Place one jet either side of the head, above the level of the ear
Place one jet either side at the top of the arms
Place one jet either side beside the feet

**What this net can be used for:**
Helping to manage resources of self and others
Encouraging a business-like approach to any project
Balancing personal emotions when the focus of others' attention

**Zodiac position**
14°05 Cancer

# Spica

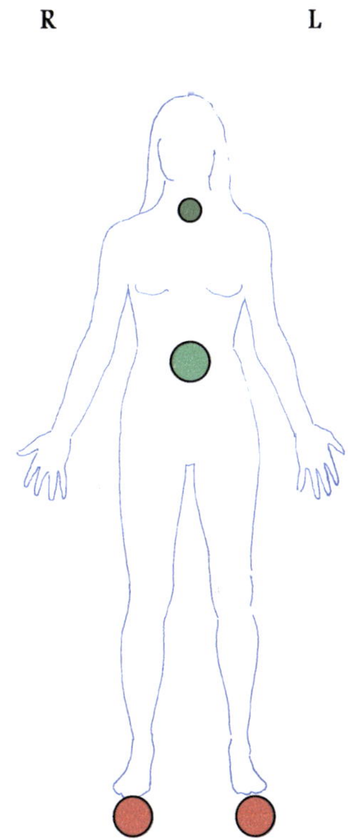


**Crystals needed:**
1 malachite
1 green aventurine
2 red garnets

**Colour of cloth to lie on:**
Black

**Placement of Stones**
Place malachite at the base of the throat
Place the green aventurine midway between the Solar Plexus and the navel
Place a red garnet in contact with the base of each foot

**What this net can be used for:**
Exploring personal creativity and artistry
Easing personal, social relationships
Encouraging contentment with one's lot in life

**Zodiac position**
23°50 Libra

# Vega

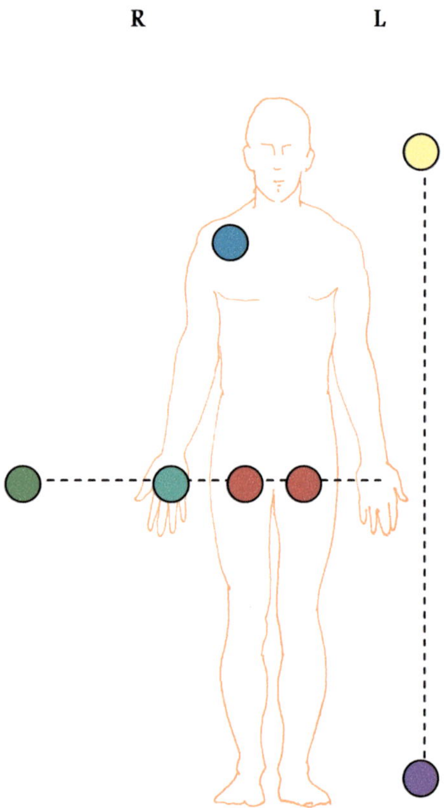


**Crystals needed:**
1 pale citrine
1 turquoise
1 aquamarine
1 green aventurine
2 red jasper
1 amethyst

**Colour of cloth to lie on:**
Yellow

**Placement of Stones**
Place the pale citrine level with the left ear, outside of the edge of the left hand
Place the turquoise at the front of the right shoulder
Place the aquamarine in the palm of the right hand
Place the green aventurine level with the stone in the right hand, but further away from the body
Place a red jasper on each of the groin points (edges of the pubic bone)
Place the amethyst beside the left foot

**What this net can be used for:**
Developing artistic and musical skills
Giving hope when all seems to be dark, depressed and empty
Reigning in excessive energy

**Zodiac position**
15°19 Capricorn

# Galactic Doorways

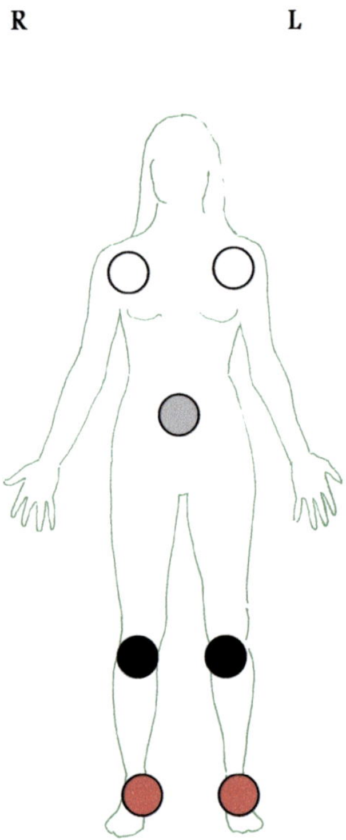


# Galactic Centre

**Crystals needed:**
2 clear selenite
1 smoky quartz
2 jet
2 red garnets

**Colour of cloth to lie on:**
Green

**Placement of Stones**
Place one clear selenite at the front of each shoulder (top of the armpit)
Place a smoky quartz at the navel
Place a piece of jet below each kneecap
Place a red garnet at the top of the arch of each foot

**What this net can be used for:**
Aligning oneself to the centre of the planet and galaxy
Activating one's life purpose
Encourages feelings of "belonging", being part of the whole

**Zodiac position**
26°58 Sagittarius

# Milky Way

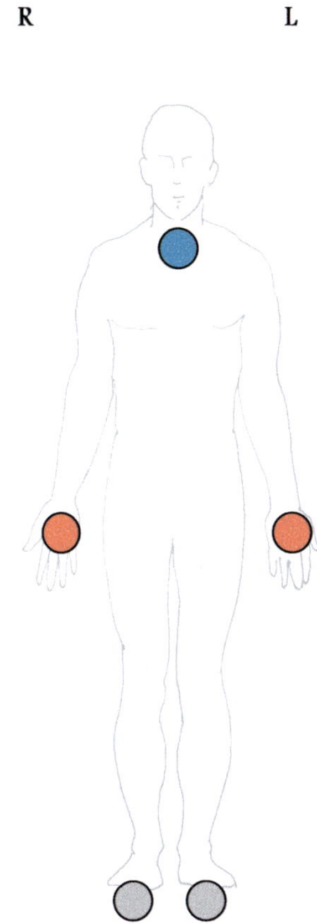


**Crystals needed:**
1 turquoise
2 carnelian
2 smoky quartz

**Colour of cloth to lie on:**
White

**Placement of Stones**
Place the turquoise at the base of the throat
Place a carnelian in each hand
Place a smoky quartz touching the base of each foot

**What this net can be used for:**
Linking with personal or collective Ancestors
Feelings of being nurtured by all creation
Helping when experiencing isolation, dissociation and loneliness

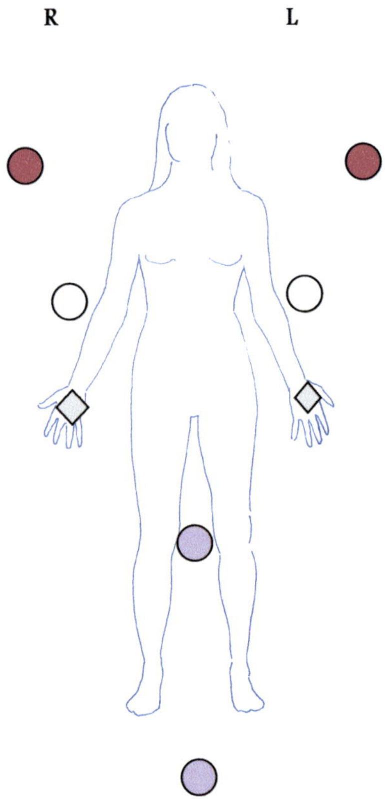


# Star Teachers

**Crystals needed:**
2 rubies
2 selenite
2 kunzite
Optional—2 personal stones

**Colour of cloth to lie on:**
Blue

**Placement of Stones**
Place a ruby each side of the body at throat level
Closer to the body at Solar Plexus level, place a selenite at either side
Place a kunzite between the legs at knee level
Place a second kunzite below the feet

Sometimes personal stones will also be needed to hold in the hands (same stone for each hand)

**What this net can be used for:**
Feelings of disconnection from people, the planet and life in general
Removing blocks to personal spiritual progress
Helps to deal with the stress of living in the world

## Star Protectors

Crystals needed:
3 turquoise
3 sodalite
1 celestite

Colour of cloth to lie on:
Indigo

Placement of Stones
Place one turquoise at the thymus, upper chest
Place a turquoise at the front of each armpit
Place a sodalite on the front of each hip bone
Place another sodalite between the legs at mid-calf level
Place a celestite at the Earth Star Chakra, midline below the feet

What this net can be used for:
Quietening personal energy, removing distractions
Anchoring the whole being into the physical body
Creating a cloak of invisibility around you

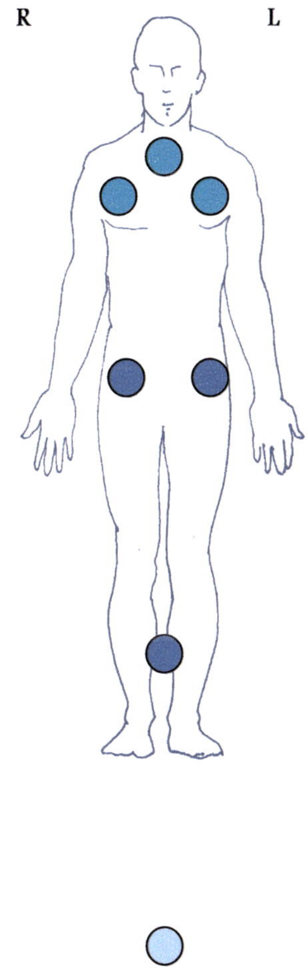

# Union with Solar System Energies

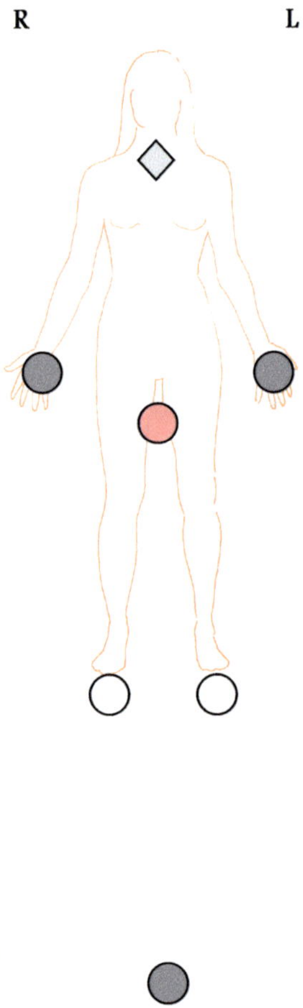


**Crystals needed:**
3 smoky quartz
2 clear quartz
1 rhodocrosite
1 personal choice

**Colour of cloth to lie on:**
Yellow

**Placement of Stones**
Place one stone at the throat chakra to suit the individual
Place a smoky quartz in each hand
Place a rhodocrosite between the legs, close to the base of the spine
Resting below each foot, close to the soles, clear quartz
Place a smoky quartz at the Earth Star chakra

**What this net can be used for:**
Understanding the processes, realities and restriction of having a physical body
Accessing deep wisdom of the Self
Acceptance of life purpose, whatever it may be

# Union with Star Realms



Crystals needed:
1 amethyst
1 turquoise
4 stones (the same) of personal choice

Colour of cloth to lie on:
Pink

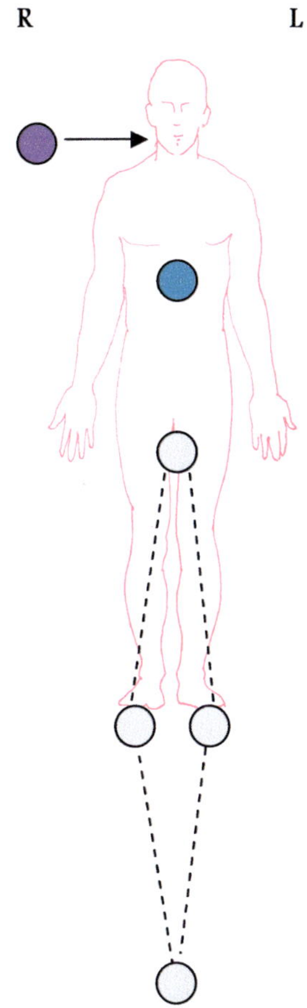


### Placement of Stones

Place the amethyst at the base of the skull (tucked behind the neck)
Place the turquoise at the base of the sternum/diaphragm level
Place four stones of the same type—a personal choice—at the base of the spine, the soles of each foot and at the Earth Star chakra

### What this net can be used for:

Acknowledging the timeless nature of the Self
A space to rest from everyday pressures of life
Reaching the deep recesses of the Self and its links to the stars

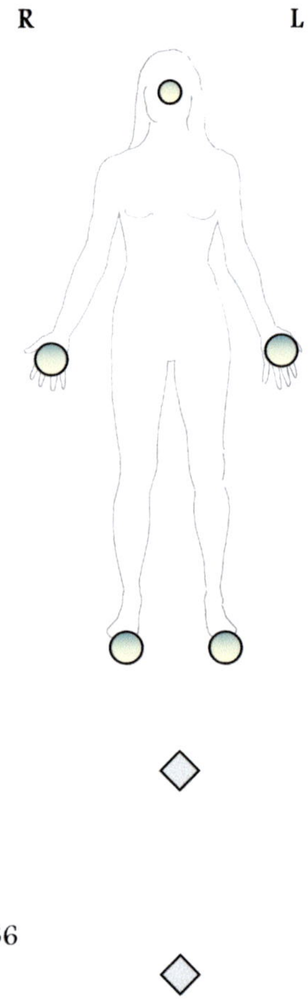


# Union with Galaxy Energies

**Crystals needed:**
5 amazonite
2 personal stones

**Colour of cloth to lie on:**
White

**Placement of Stones**
Place one amazonite close to the bridge of the nose
Place one amazonite in each hand
Place one amazonite in contact with the sole of each foot
Place one personal stone at earth star chakra
Place one other personal stone at the midline as far from the body as possible below the Earth Star stone

**What this net can be used for:**
Aligning to the over-lighting subtle energies of the galaxy
Recognition of the coherence of patterns from many lives
Acceptance of deeper flows of life-force that connect us to other parts of our being

# Union with Universal Energies



Crystals needed:
2 personal stones
2 amethyst
2 obsidian
2 clear quartz

Colour of cloth to lie on:
Yellow

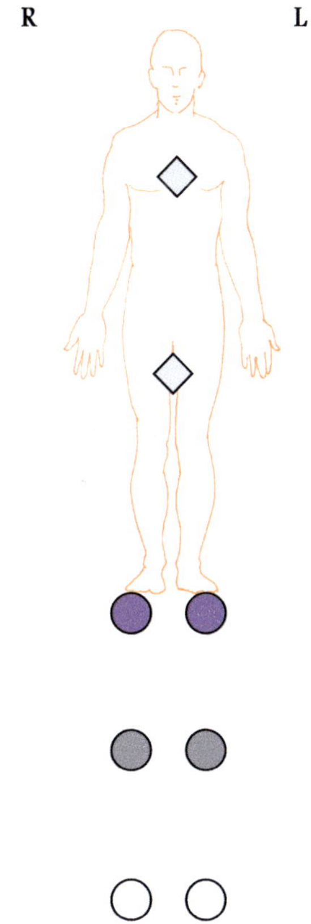


Placement of Stones
Personal choice of stone at the Heart Chakra (centre of chest)
Personal choice of stone at the Root chakra (base of spine)
Place an amethyst below each foot
2ft/40cms below these on the same line, obsidian
2ft/40cms below these on the same line, clear quartz

What this net can be used for:
Accepting nurturing energies from all levels of consciousness
Understanding the continuity of life
Acceptance of self in the wider scheme of things

# Personal Doorways

Personal

# Subtle Vision

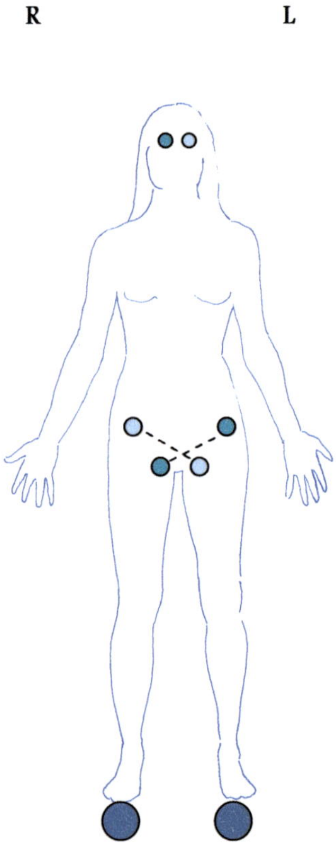


**Crystals needed:**
3 celestite
3 turquoise
2 sapphire

**Colour of cloth to lie on:**
Blue

**Placement of Stones**
Above the left eye, place a celestite
Above the right eye, place a turquoise
At the Root chakra, on the groin points:
Place a celestite on the left, with a turquoise above it
Place a turquoise on the right, with a celestite above it
Place a sapphire touching the sole of each foot

**What this net can be used for:**
Removing blocks to new levels of perception
Balances the lateral energies of the body and brain
Relaxation into body awareness, allowing deep flows of communication

# Source of Power



Crystals needed:
1 dark carnelian
3 lapis lazuli

Colour of cloth to lie on:
Violet

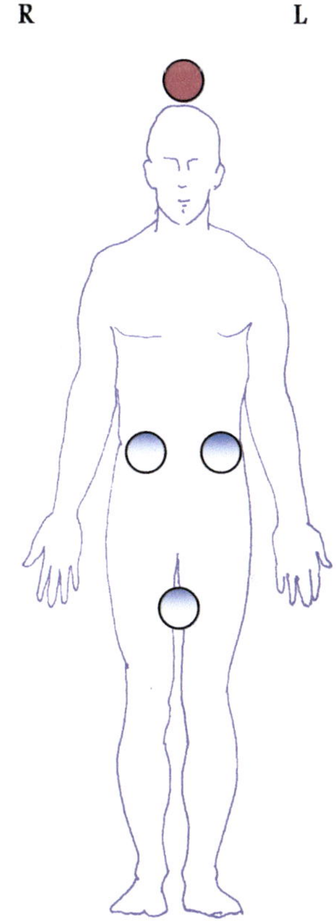


Placement of Stones
Place the dark carnelian in contact with the top of the head
Place a lapis lazuli either side of the navel
Place a lapis lazuli near the base of the spine

What this net can be used for:
Integrating personal energies into the physical body
Increase in flow of communication between all layers of the aura
Accessing energy from other lives

Personal

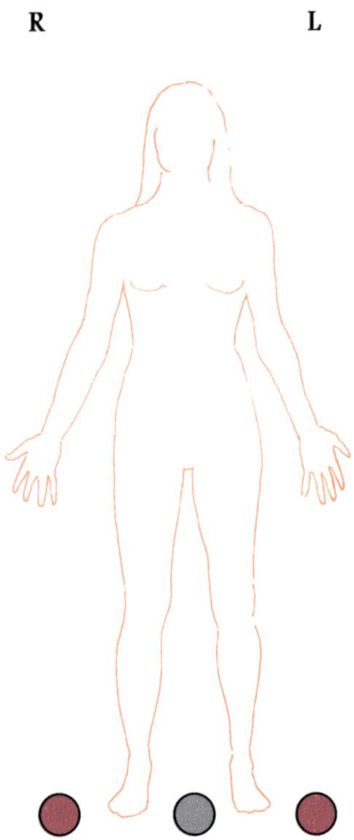


# Integration of Past, Present and Future

**Crystals needed:**
1 haematite
2 rubies

**Colour of cloth to lie on:**
Orange

**Placement of Stones**
All the stones are in a line with the stone between the feet—the haematite
Place a ruby outside each foot

When the process is complete, hold a clear quartz in the hands for the same length of time as you were in the net

**What this net can be used for:**
Focusing dispersed energy from other lives
Preparing for a spiritual quest
Final stages of recovery from long illness or deep shock

# Teacher Doorways

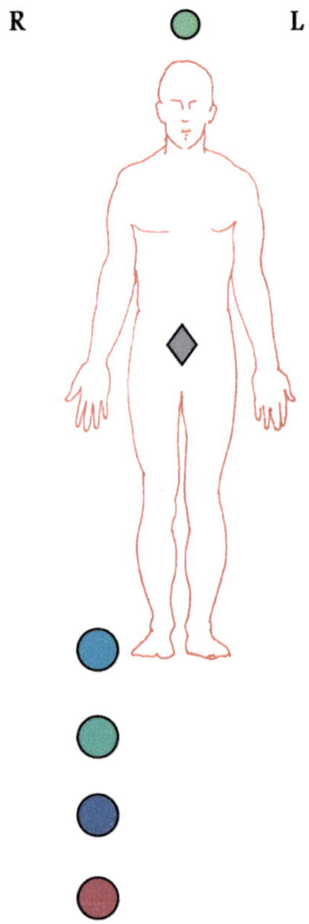


# Teachers of the Animal Kingdom

**Crystals needed:**
1 emerald
1 turquoise
1 aquamarine
1 lapis lazuli
1 red garnet
1 personal stone

**Colour of cloth to lie on:**
Red

**Placement of Stones**
Place the emerald, midline above the head
Choice of personal crystal at the second chakra
Place the turquoise beside the right foot
Place the aquamarine, 1 ft/20cms below that
Place the lapis lazuli, 1 ft/20cms below that
Place the red garnet, 1 ft/20cms below that

**What this net can be used for:**
Linking to power animals and spirit animal guardians
Communication and empathy with animal consciousness
Settling into body consciousness, increasing intuitive awareness

# Teachers of the Mineral Kingdom

**Crystals needed:**
1 personal stone
1 rhodonite
1 amethyst
2 black tourmaline
1 olivine
1 sodalite
1 clear quartz

**Colour of cloth to lie on:**
Orange

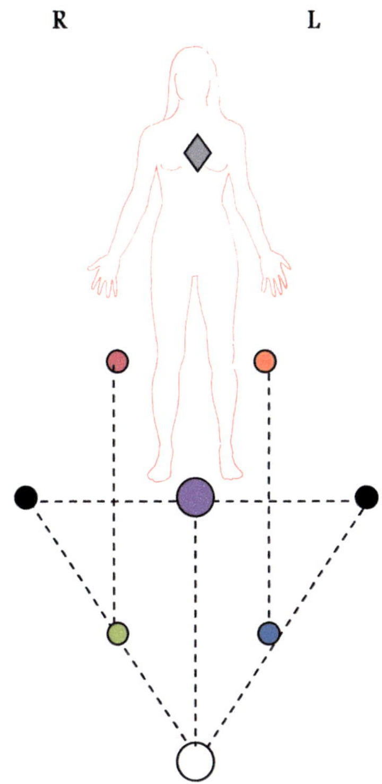


**Placement of Stones**
Place a personal stone of choice at the heart chakra to align the person to the net energies
Place a rhodonite on the right at knee level
Place a carnelian on the left at knee level
Place the amethyst below the feet, on the midline
Place a black tourmaline on either side of this, away from the body
Place the olivine, in line with the rhodonite, below and away from the feet
Place the sodalite, in line with the olivine on the left
Place the clear quartz at the Earth Star chakra

**What this net can be used for:**
Communication and teaching from deep structures of the Earth and Universe
Opening to deep time
Grounding, harmony with Earth energies

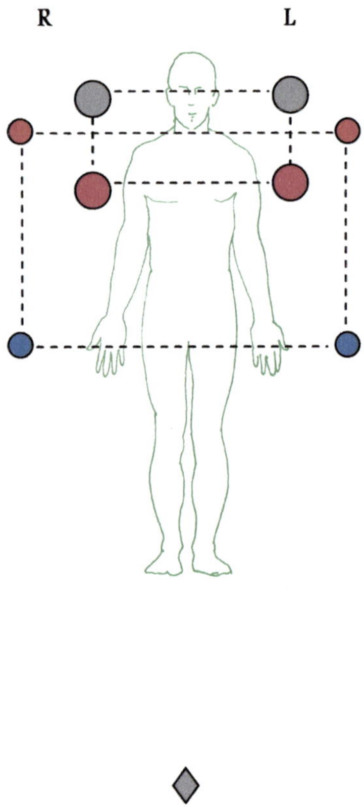


# Teachers of the Plant Kingdom

**Crystals needed:**
2 smoky quartz
2 red jasper
2 red garnet
2 sodalite
1 personal stone

**Colour of cloth to lie on:**
Green

**Placement of Stones**
Place the smoky quartz either side of the ears
Level with the throat, place the red jaspers either side, further away from the body than the smoky quartz
Level with the heart in line with the smoky quartz, place a red garnet either side
Place sodalite level with each hand and in line with the red jaspers
Place the personal stone at the Earth Star chakra

**What this net can be used for:**
Helping to link to plant spirits and the consciousness of the plant kingdom
Understanding the healing and spiritual qualities of plants
Harmony with the forces of Nature

# Teachers of the Lower World



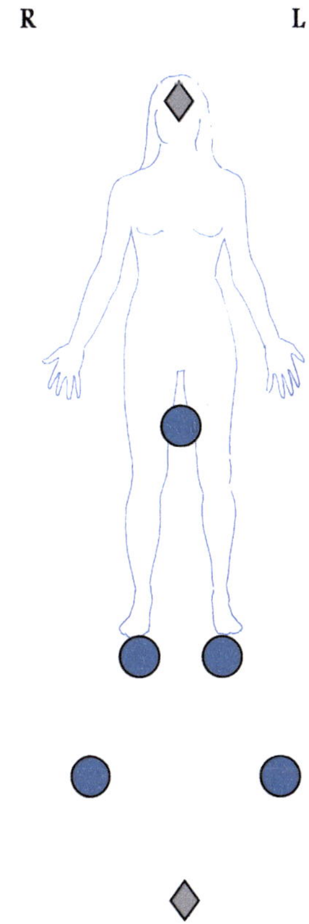


Crystals needed:
5 lapis lazuli
1 clear quartz point
1 personal stone

Colour of cloth to lie on:
Indigo

Placement of Stones
Place the personal choice stone on the centre of the forehead (the brow chakra)
Place one lapis lazuli close to the base of the spine
Place one lapis lazuli below the centre of each foot
Below these place another , away from each side of the body
Place the clear quartz point along the midline as far as possible away from the body, point towards the body if terminated

What this net can be used for:
Accessing personal power
Ancestral contacts
Sources of energy
Understanding the foundations of all things
Meeting Lower World teachers and guides

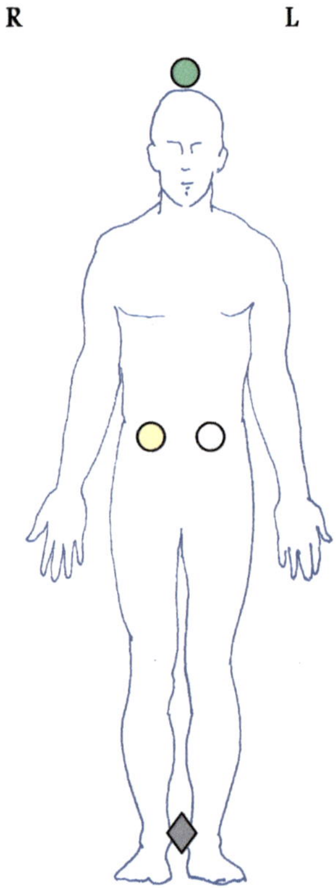


# Middle World Teachers

**Crystals needed:**
1 ruby
1 clear quartz
1 pearl
1 personal choice stone

**Colour of cloth to lie on:**
Indigo

**Placement of Stones**
Place the ruby touching the top of the head
Place the pearl beside the right side of the navel
Place the clear quartz beside the left side of the navel
Place the personal stone, between the legs at ankle level

**What this net can be used for:**
Reconnection to subtle levels of information
Increased awareness and perception of energies
Spiritual teachers and guardians

# Teachers of the Upper World



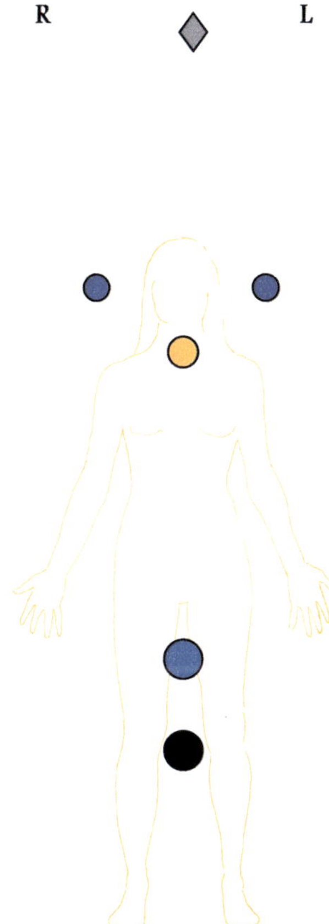


Crystals needed:
3 lapis lazuli
1 citrine
1 black tourmaline
1 personal stone

Colour of cloth to lie on:
Yellow

**Placement of Stones**

Place two lapis lazuli on either side of the head, just above the ears and in line with the shoulders
Place the citrine at the throat chakra
Place a lapis lazuli at the base of the spine (root chakra)
Place the black tourmaline between the knees on the midline
Place the personal stone as far above the head as possible, on the midline

What this net can be used for:
Connecting with levels of clarity and intelligence
Understanding of relationship between beings
Contacting teachers and guides

# Tree Doorways

# Accessing Tree Kingdoms

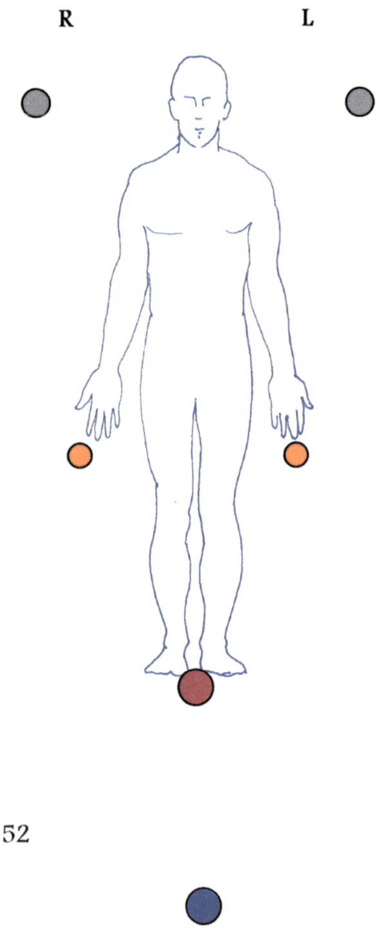


**Crystals needed:**
1 ruby
1 sapphire
2 carnelian
2 lodestone

**Colour of cloth to lie on:**
Indigo

**Placement of Stones**
Place the ruby midline between the feet
Place the sapphire at the Earth Star chakra
Place a carnelian beside each hand
Further out than the carnelians, at the level of the ears, place the lodestones, one on each side

**What this net can be used for:**
Becoming aligned to spiritual energy of tree consciousness
Awareness of deep levels of interaction and harmony
Increased sensitivity to allow effective working with tree spirits

# Lord of the Forest

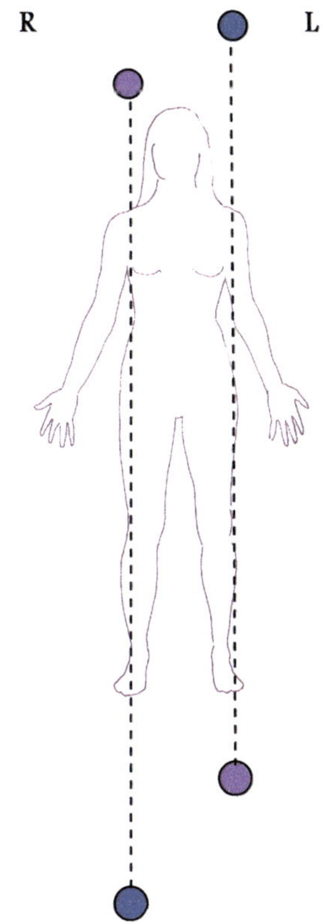


**Crystals needed:**
2 amethyst
2 sodalite

**Colour of cloth to lie on:**
Violet

**Placement of Stones**
Place one amethyst on a line with the right shoulder, above the head level
Place a sodalite on a line with the left ear, above the level of the amethyst
Place a sodalite under the right foot, but away from the body
Place a piece of amethyst under the left foot

**What this net can be used for:**
Contact with archetypal and ancestral consciousness of forest ecology
Increased relationship with Earth soul
Awareness of spirit realms within physical existence

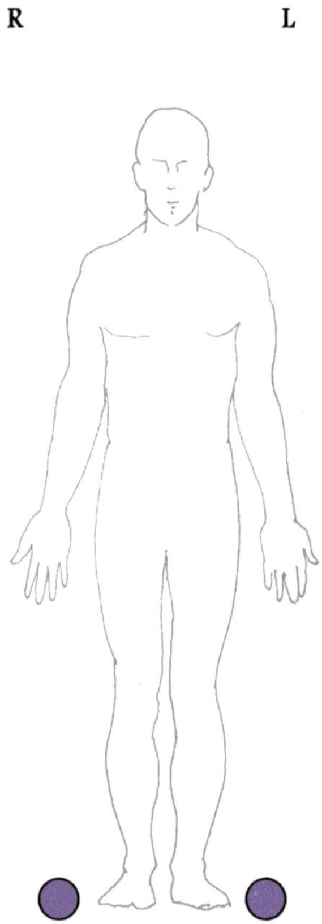


## Aspen (Populus tremula)

**Crystals needed:**
2 amethyst

**Colour of cloth to lie on:**
White

**Placement of Stones**
Place amethyst on the beside the feet

**What this net can be used for:**
Bringing personal wisdom to the fore
Calming fears by allowing broader perspective
Encouraging humour and amusement

# Black Poplar (Populus nigra)



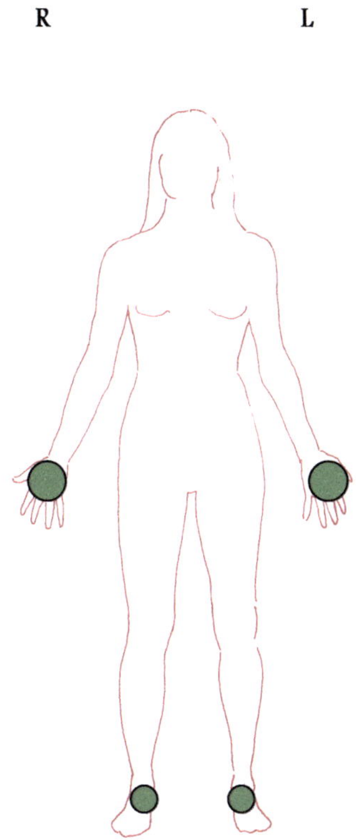


**Crystals needed:**
4 green jaspers

**Colour of cloth to lie on:**
Dark Red

**Placement of Stones**
Place one green jasper in each hand
Place one green jasper on the top of each instep on the feet

**What this net can be used for:**
Strengthening the immune system
Linking subtle bodies with the physical
Increasing confidence and security

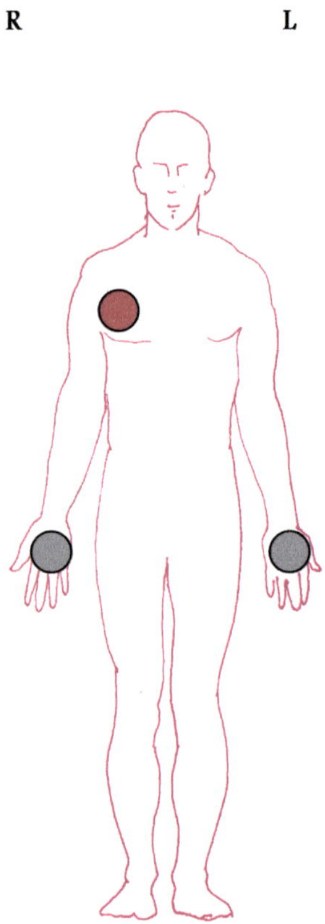


# Elder (Sambucus nigra)

**Crystals needed:**
1 red amber
2 smoky quartz

**Colour of cloth to lie on:**
Pink

**Placement of Stones**
Place the red amber on the right side of the chest, level with the armpit
Place a smoky quartz in each hand

**What this net can be used for:**
Soothes difficult and destructive emotions
Increases self-worth and self-tolerance
Enables insight into emotions and personal reactions

# English Elm (Ulmus procera)

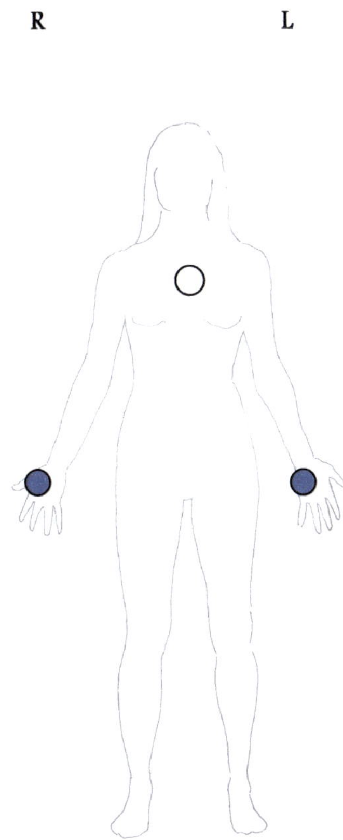


**Crystals needed:**
1 white/clear fluorite
2 azurite

**Colour of cloth to lie on:**
White

**Placement of Stones**
Place the white/clear fluorite at the heart centre
Place an azurite in each hand

**What this net can be used for:**
Increasing fine levels of communication
Protection by quietening personal energies
Balancing chakras to create easy flow of inner communication

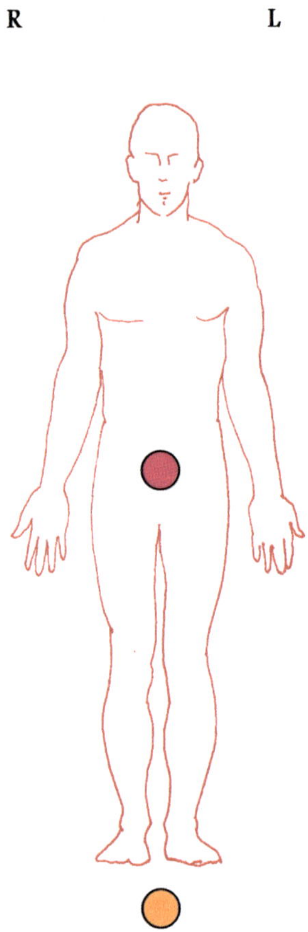


# Gean, Wild Cherry (Prunus avium)

**Crystals needed:**
1 cherry opal
1 citrine point

**Colour of cloth to lie on:**
Red

**Placement of Stones**
Place the cherry opal at the second chakra
Place the citrine, point down, between the feet

**What this net can be used for:**
Soothing irritation, pain and inflammation
Activating of healing processes
Clearing of subtle energy channels of the body

## Glastonbury Thorn (Crataegus monogyna biflora)

**Crystals needed:**
1 ruby
12 clear quartz

**Colour of cloth to lie on:**
Violet

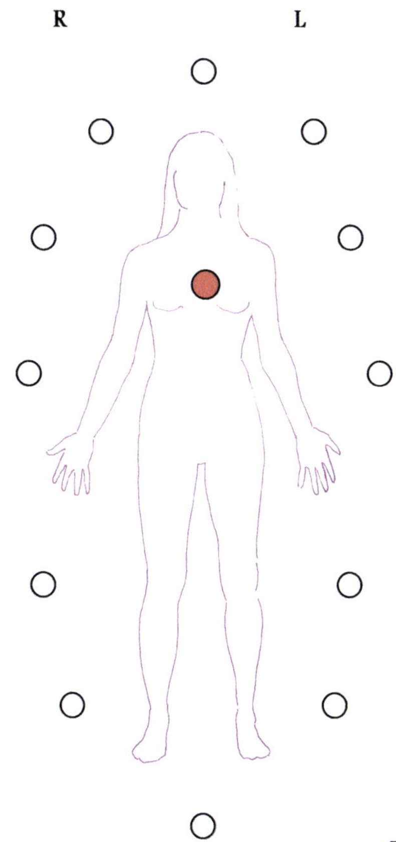


**Placement of Stones**
Place the ruby at the heart centre
Place the clear quartz evenly spaced around the body

**What this net can be used for:**
Clarifying personal direction in life
Releasing blocked energies from the heart chakra
Relaxation into states where intuition is increased

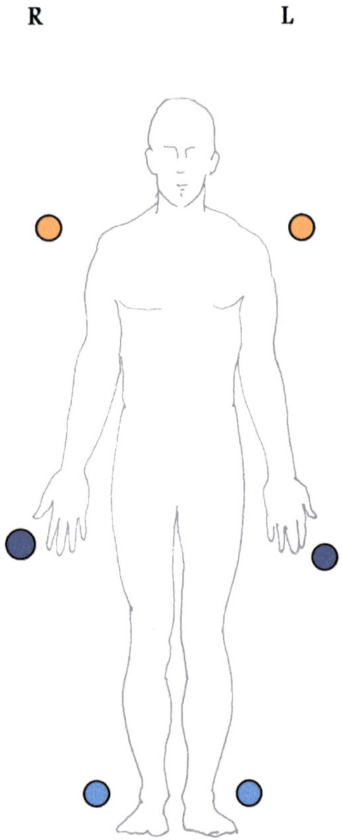


# Hazel (Corylus avellana)

**Crystals needed:**
2 lapis lazuli
2 amber
2 blue fluorite

**Colour of cloth to lie on:**
White

**Placement of Stones**
Place two amber on either side of the shoulders
Place a lapis lazuli by the fingers of each hand
Place a blue fluorite by each ankle

**What this net can be used for:**
Developing personal skills
Giving and receiving wisdom and information
Stabilises energy and focuses in the Now

# Holm Oak (Quercus ilex)

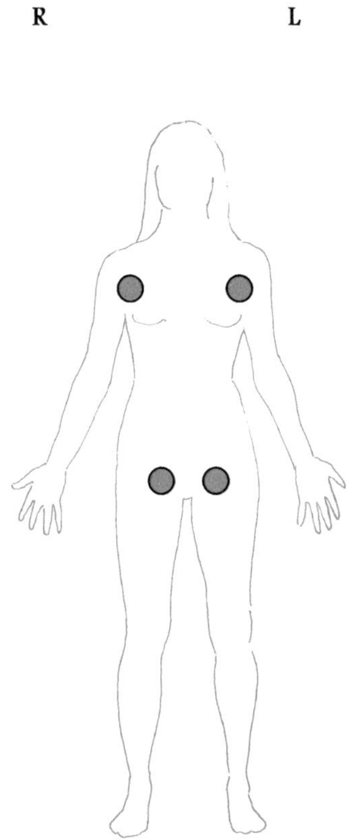


**Crystals needed:**
4 green aventurine

**Colour of cloth to lie on:**
Green

**Placement of Stones**
Place a green aventurine on each groin point (edges of the pubic bone
Place a green aventurine on the front of each armpit

**What this net can be used for:**
Dispelling negative emotions
Encouraging expression of personal beliefs
Increases capacity to deal with disruptions and dissonant energies

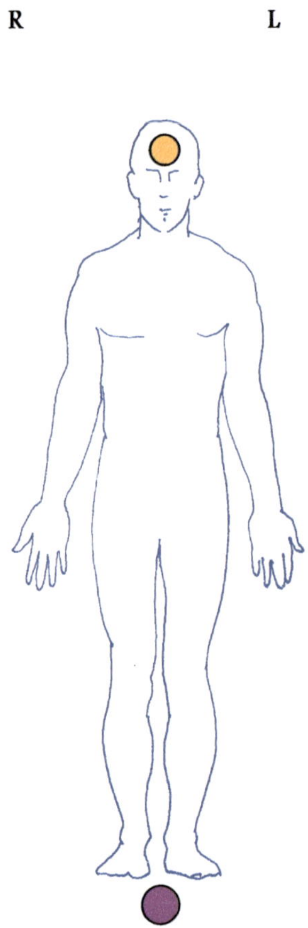


# Juniper (Juniperus communis)

**Crystals needed:**
1 citrine
1 amethyst

**Colour of cloth to lie on:**
Indigo

**Placement of Stones**
Place the citrine on the forehead
Place the amethyst between the feet

**What this net can be used for:**
Cleansing all levels of the aura
Stabilises energies allowing them to strengthen the physical body
Helping to release difficulties from the past

# Medlar (Mespilus germanicus)



**Crystals needed:**
1 citrine
1 clear calcite
(Iceland spar)

**Colour of cloth to lie on:**
Pink

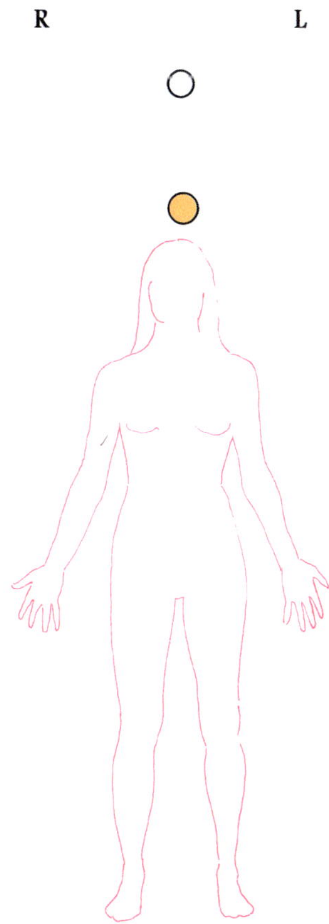


**Placement of Stones**
Place the citrine at the top of the head
Place the clear calcite above the citrine, on the midline

**What this net can be used for:**
Increasing joy and happiness
Expansion of view, allowing a broader context for personal issues
Confidence and inner contentment

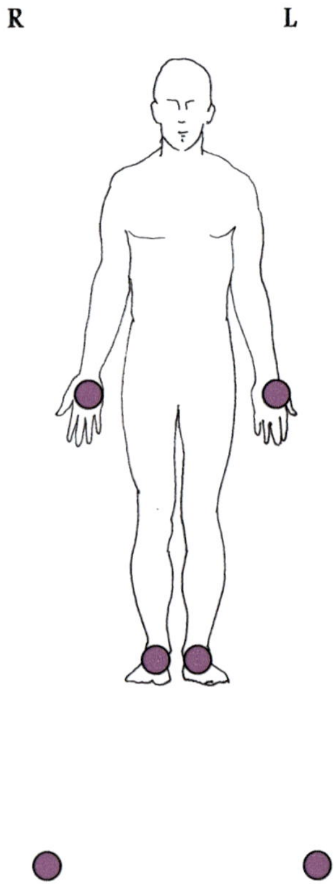


# Persian Ironwood (Parrotia persica)

**Crystals needed:**
6 amethyst

**Colour of cloth to lie on:**
Black

**Placement of Stones**
Place an amethyst in each hand
Place an amethyst on the arch of each foot
Place an amethyst below each foot, further out than the other stones

**What this net can be used for:**
Deep grounding and access to life-force
Stabilising energies through difficult life experiences
Increasing sense of security

# Pittospora (Kohuhu) (Pittosporum tenuifolium)

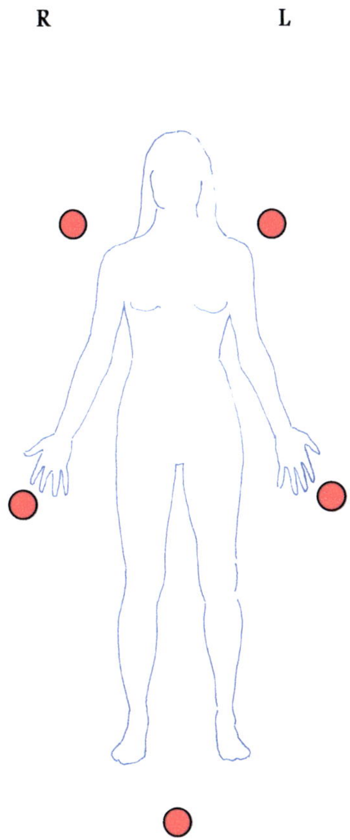


**Crystals needed:**
5 rhodocrosite

**Colour of cloth to lie on:**
Blue

**Placement of Stones**
Place the rhodocrosites around the body in an inverted pentagram (beside the shoulders, hips and below and between the feet)

**What this net can be used for:**
Helping decision making
Increasing clarity at all levels of perception
Dissolves solemnity and seriousness

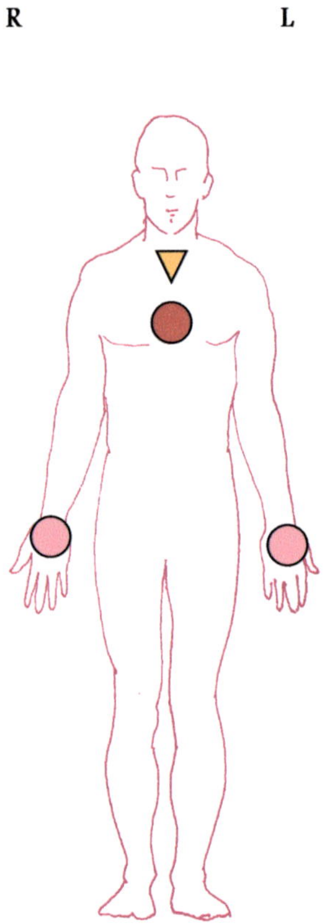


## Silver Birch (Betula pendula)

**Crystals needed:**
1 citrine point
2 rose quartz
1 red granite

**Colour of cloth to lie on:**
Red or Pink

**Placement of Stones**
Place a rose quartz in both hands
Place the citrine, point down, at the sternal notch
Place red granite at the centre of the chest

**What this net can be used for:**
Enhancing experience of beauty and simplicity
Initiating new activities and projects
Increases acceptance, reducing tendencies to judge harshly

# Tulip Tree (Liridendron tulipifera)

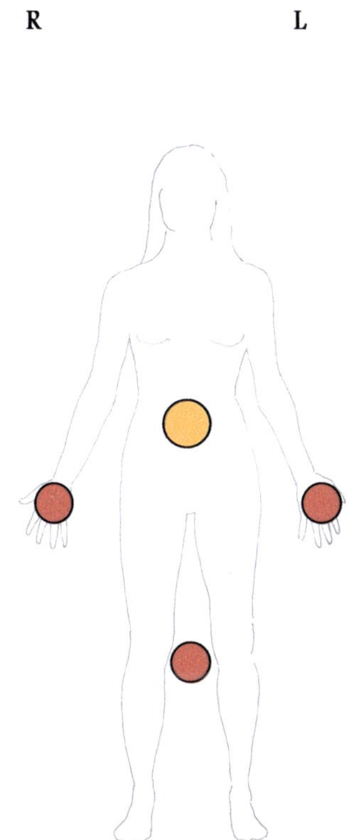


**Crystals needed:**
1 citrine
3 red jasper

**Colour of cloth to lie on:**
White

**Placement of Stones**
Place the citrine at the solar plexus
Place a red jasper in each hand and one between the knees

**What this net can be used for:**
Encouraging practical outlets for spiritual processes and ideas
Relaxing the digestive organs increasing nourishment and satiety
Increasing feelings of peace and contentment

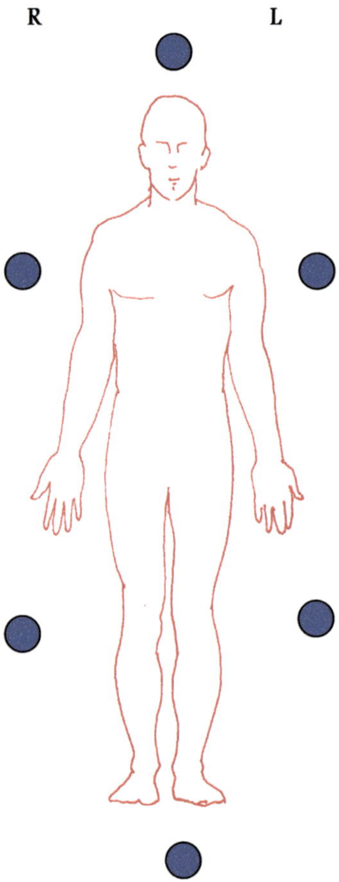


# Wayfaring Tree (Viburnum lantana)

**Crystals needed:**
6 lapis lazuli

**Colour of cloth to lie on:**
Red

**Placement of Stones**
Place the lapis lazuli evenly spaced around the body

**What this net can be used for:**
Accessing far memory for personal and environmental information
Reinforcing emotional boundaries
Interlacing emotions from several sources into a coherent pattern

# Profound Patterns

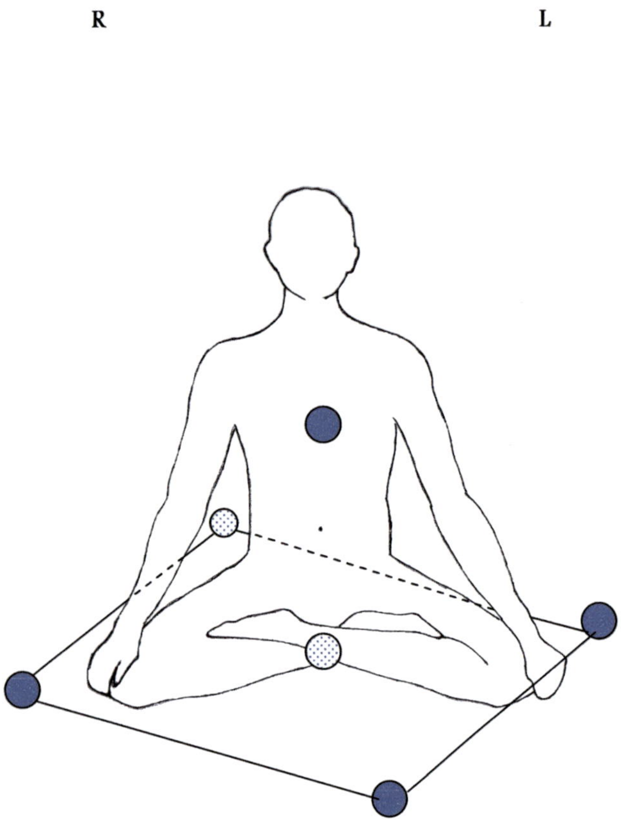


## Balancing the Elements

Placements

The placements shown can be anything that carries and energy signature:
Crystal, Essence
Colour, Rune
Leaf, flower, fruit, twig
Essential oil

These can be chosen intuitively by yourself or your client, by dowsing or muscle-testing

**What this pattern can be used for:**
Integrating elements within the individual and between the individual and the world.
Bringing harmony between the individual and the environment.

This process works best when the individual is allowed to chose the direction that they face

# Diamond Sky



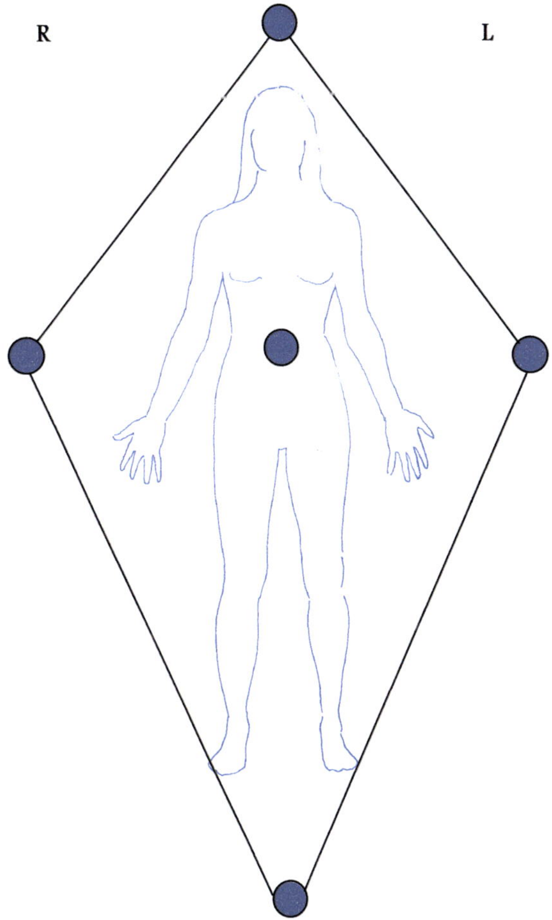


Placements

The placements shown can be anything that carries and energy signature:
Crystal, Essence
Colour, Rune
Leaf, flower, fruit, twig
Essential oil

These can be chosen intuitively by yourself or your client, by dowsing or muscle-testing

**What this pattern can be used for:**
Creating a safe healing space for the energies of the central item to be accessed and integrated.

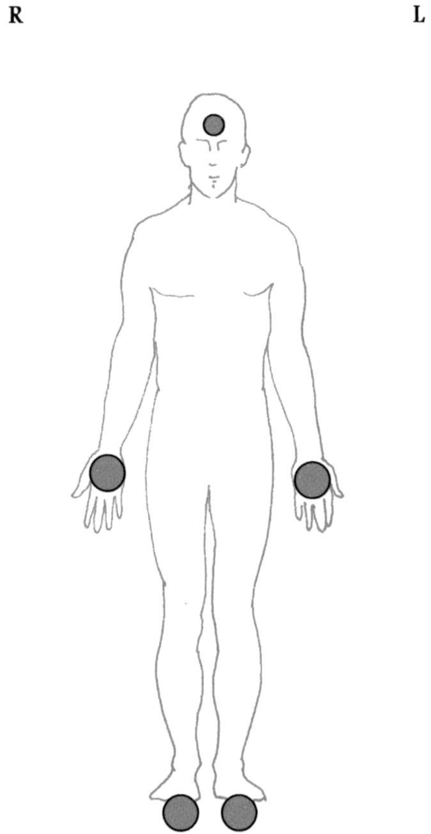




# Druid's Foot

### Placements

The placements shown can be anything that carries and energy signature:
Crystal, Essence
Colour, Rune
Leaf, flower, fruit, twig
Essential oil

These can be chosen intuitively by yourself or your client, by dowsing or muscle-testing

**What this pattern can be used for:**
Re-focusing and redefining personal space and activity
Dealing with feelings of being 'strung out'
Easing the experience of lack of direction or motivation

# Mirror Body



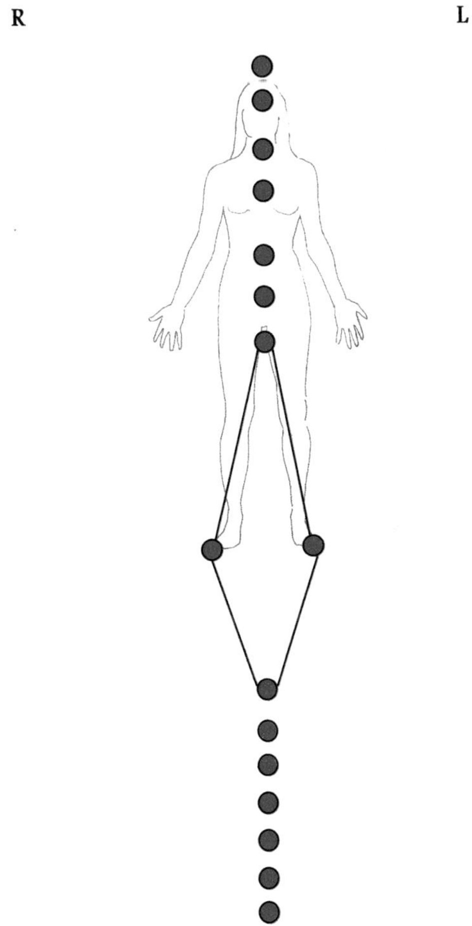


## Placements

The placements shown can be anything that carries and energy signature:
Crystal, Essence
Colour, Rune
Leaf, flower, fruit, twig
Essential oil

These can be chosen intuitively by yourself or your client, by dowsing or muscle-testing

**What this pattern can be used for:**
Centring and grounding
Integrating disparate energies and focus
Easing feelings of alienation

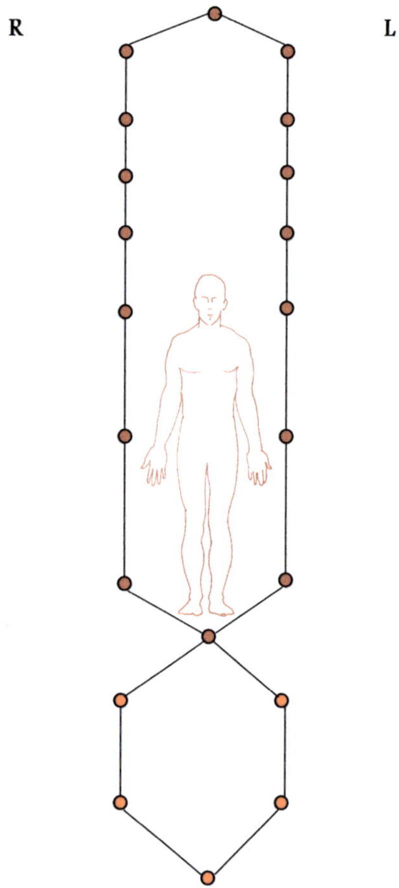


# Spirit Road

## Placements

The placements shown can be anything that carries and energy signature:
Crystal, Essence
Colour, Rune
Leaf, flower, fruit, twig
Essential oil

These can be chosen intuitively by yourself or your client, by dowsing or muscle-testing

**What this pattern can be used for:**
Using a goal, this net can be directed as required. The space available will define the length of the 'road'

Not all the points indicated will necessarily need something placed on them

# Three Trees

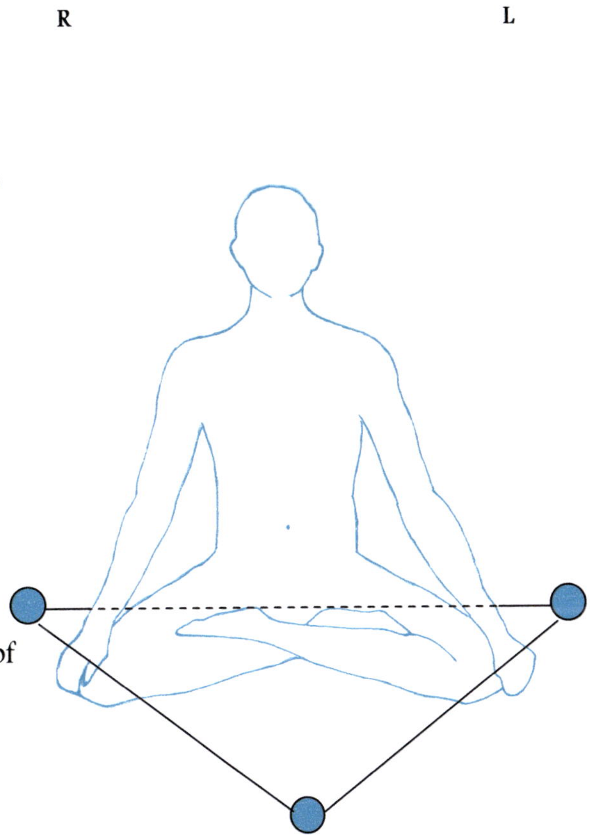


## Placements

The placements shown can be anything that carries and energy signature:
Crystal, Essence
Colour, Rune
Leaf, flower, fruit, twig
Essential oil

These can be chosen intuitively by yourself or your client, by dowsing or muscle-testing

**What this pattern can be used for:**
Realigning the individual when there is a loss of one's centre
Easing acceptance of difficulties in life
Supporting the individual when there are feelings of 'being stuck between a rock and a hard place'
Creating stability and solidity

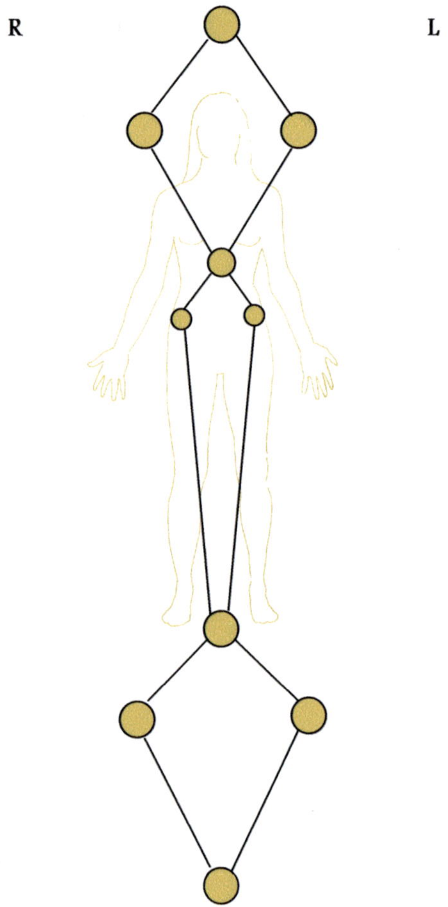


# Three Worlds

## Placements

The placements shown can be anything that carries and energy signature:
Crystal, Essence
Colour, Rune
Leaf, flower, fruit, twig
Essential oil

These can be chosen intuitively by yourself or your client, by dowsing or muscle-testing

**What this pattern can be used for:**
Increasing grounding and connect with the planet
Focusing personal energy
Deep healing of solar plexus chakra issues
Aiding personal power, stability

# Time Clearing



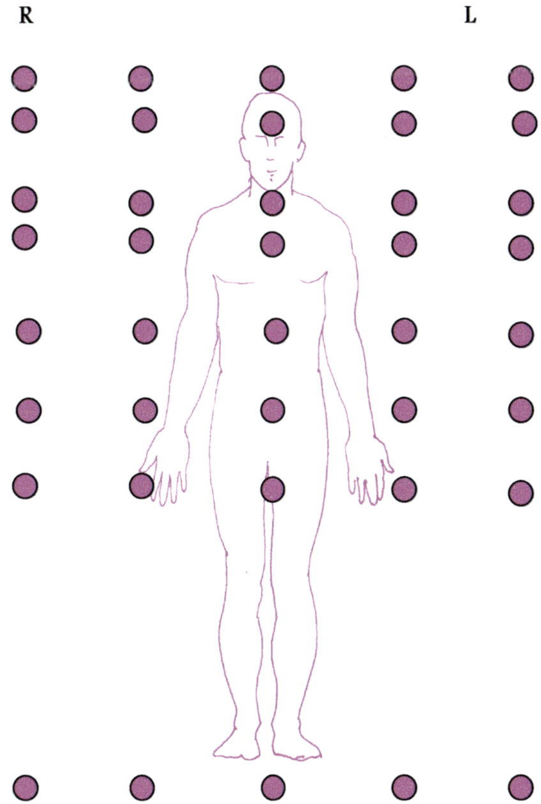


## Placements

The placements shown can be anything that carries and energy signature:
Crystal, Essence
Colour, Rune
Leaf, flower, fruit, twig
Essential oil

These can be chosen intuitively by yourself or your client, by dowsing or muscle-testing

Not all places require items.

**What this pattern can be used for:**
Dealing with persistent or chronic imbalances
Clearing repetitive patterns, symptoms
Shifting blocks that have been held for many life-times

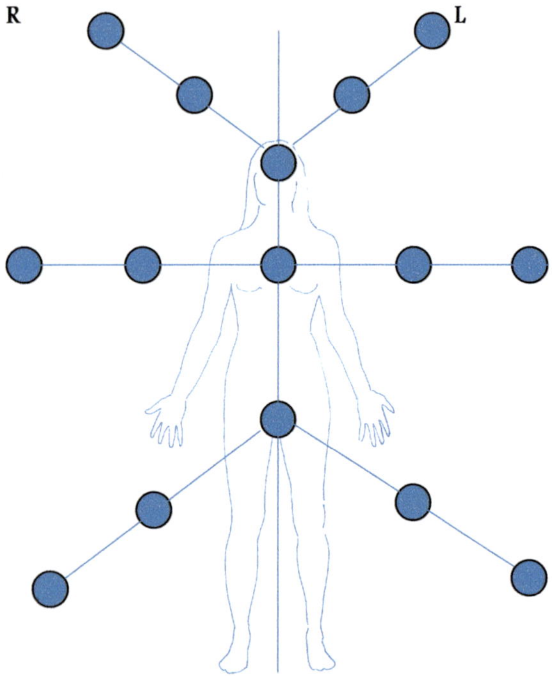


# World Tree

## Placements

The placements shown can be anything that carries and energy signature:
Crystal, Essence
Colour, Rune
Leaf, flower, fruit, twig
Essential oil

These can be chosen intuitively by yourself or your client, by dowsing or muscle-testing

**What this pattern can be used for:**
Integrating different levels of the individual by accessing different dimensions
Grounding
Protecting

# Energies of the Land

## Land Energies

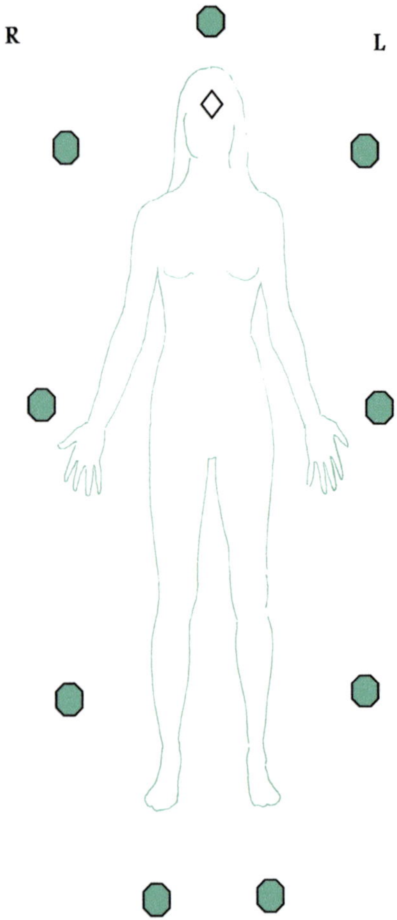


# Earth Goddess

**Crystals needed:**
9 labradorite
1 herkimer diamond

**Colour of cloth to lie on:**
Green

**Placement of Stones**
9 labradorite tumbles, evenly spaced
1 herkimer diamond on the brow
(Optional—black tourmaline centrally, below the feet)

**What this pattern can be used for:**
Feelings of disconnection from life, insecure, isolated, overwhelmed or ungrounded.
Reconnecting to the planet,
Personal energies on every level become stabilised.
Creating extra clarity in our thinking to see through the illusions around us and to what we can do to make a difference.

# The Merlin

**Crystals needed:**
1 herkimer diamond
1 kyanite
1 black tourmaline

**Colour of cloth to lie on:**
Indigo

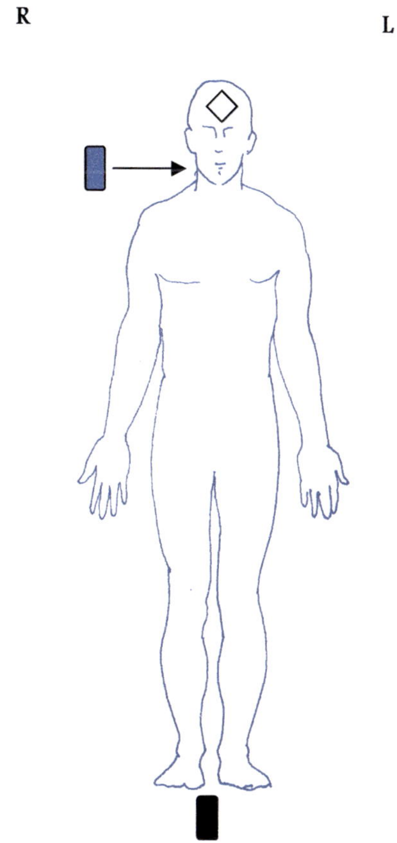


**Placement of Stones**
1 herkimer diamond on the brow
1 Kyanite blade placed lengthwise at the occiput
(base of back of skull)
1 black tourmaline centrally, below the feet

**What this pattern can be used for:**
Feelings of being engulfed by frustration
Energies that are blocked at any level
Creating a flow of energy that can be accessed and directed to where it is needed
Appreciating ourselves, self-confidence and an increase in self-worth.
Bringing hope that we may be able to find worth and treasure when we look inside ourselves.

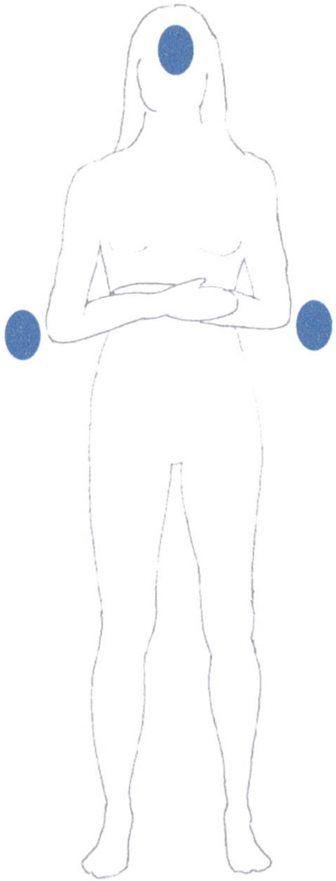


# Preseli Time-shift

**Crystals needed:**
3 Preseli bluestones
or 3 Preseli bluestone essence drops

**Colour of cloth to lie on:**
Dowse to find appropriate colour

**Placement of Stones**
One stone/drop at the Soma Chakra, above the centre of the forehead at the hairline.

Hands resting on the Solar Plexus chakra, a stone/drop by each elbow

**What this pattern can be used for:**
For access to deep levels of healing and perception of patterns associated with disease states.

# Preseli Anchor

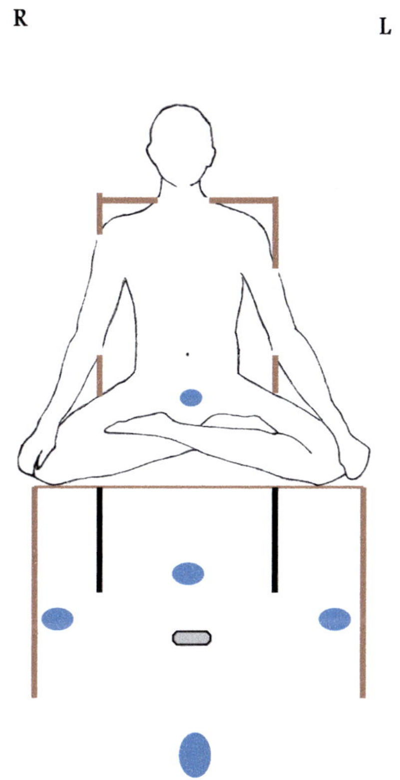


**Crystals needed:**
5 Preseli bluestone or
drops of Preseli Bluestone
essence
1 piece of natural chalk

Chair to sit on

**Placement of Stones**
Four pieces of Preseli bluestone/drops on the floor around a chair, in North, South, East and West directions
One piece of natural chalk, beneath the chair
One piece of Preseli bluestone/drop held in the hands

**What this pattern can be used for:**

Realignment of personal energies to those of universal Patterns, particularly of time, to focus healing and presence in the Now.

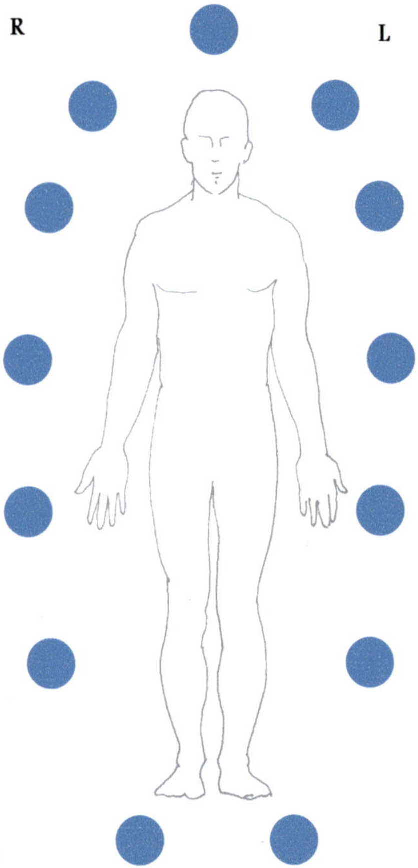


# Preseli Clear

**Crystals needed:**
13 Preseli bluestones or drops of bluestone essence

**Colour of cloth to lie on:**
White

**Placement of Stones**
Align the main axis of the body to the North/south directions, with the head to the North.
Place 13 stones around the body

**What this pattern can be used for:**
Access to subtle layers of experience and information to enhance intuition and clear levels of perception

# Useful Information:

**www.greenmanshop.co.uk**

Green Man Essences for many types of traditionally made essences, other books by Simon & Sue Lilly, sacred jewellery, music for meditation, Fine Art Prints, runes and talismans, energy healing tools and much more!

**www.mcscourses.co.uk**

Mandala Complementary Studies (MCS) for tutored and correspondence courses – crystal healing, colour therapy, essence courses, astrology, spiritual development courses, rune courses, anatomy & physiology courses. MCS is a National Open College Network Centre, so presents courses of excellent educational quality, taught by experienced tutors. Sue Lilly is the centre manager.

**www.icgt.co.uk**

Established in 1985, ICGT – the Institute of Crystal and Gem Therapists is one of the oldest crystal healing schools in the UK. ICGT provides practical, grounded courses in crystal healing and therapy to certificate and diploma levels.

**www.treeseer.com**

Website for CD downloads and individual tracks, plus the free, online Tree Spirit Oracle

Beyond Crystal Doorways £6.99
ISBN 9781905454051

9 781905 454051